Serving the Street

Serving the Street

Volunteering as Charity, Racial
Justice, and Poverty Tourism

Matthew Jerome Schneider

The University of Georgia Press
ATHENS

Sociology of Race and
Ethnicity web page

EU Authorized Representative
Easy Access System Europe—Mustamäe tee 50, 10621
Tallinn, Estonia, gpsr.requests@easproject.com

Library of Congress Control Number: 2025040261
ISBN: 9780820366388 (hardcover)
ISBN: 9780820375373 (paperback)
ISBN: 9780820375380 (epub)
ISBN: 9780820375397 (PDF)

CONTENTS

ILLUSTRATIONS

TABLES

ACKNOWLEDGMENTS

More than any other project, this book has defined the first stage of my career and now serves as a material artifact representing my growth as a scholar. The seeds of this project, truthfully, were planted when I was an undergraduate who was deeply (if unreflexively) committed to community engagement and service learning, and from there it grew into a research project at the University of Illinois at Urbana-Champaign. This project was molded further by my experiences at the University of North Carolina at Pembroke, where I began to think critically about forms of community and civic engagement that might live up to their stated goals. Ultimately, this book project brought me to the University of North Carolina Wilmington and to a department whose central mission is one of public and applied sociology. While I will certainly continue to grow as a scholar, this project has reached a stage where it is ready to be shared with others on their own paths of personal, academic, and professional development.

This book and my own development did not happen without an incredible amount of support. This book owes its existence to the many people who guided me down the path toward graduate school, toward reflection on racial and class inequalities, and toward community service and activism. In this regard, I feel lucky to have parents who taught me to care about others and to think critically about the world around me. I feel similarly lucky to have had undergraduate mentors at Illinois College, including Kelly Dagan, Richard Maye, Bob Kunath, Steve Hochstadt, and Elizabeth Rellinger, who encouraged me to do the same and who made the path to and beyond graduate school feel possible.

At the University of Illinois at Urbana-Champaign, this project was greatly impacted by my longtime adviser and director of research, Monica McDermott, who invested uncountable hours in my development as a scholar of race and racism and in the development of this project. I am also deeply indebted to Tim Liao for the support he has shown me and for teaching me how to navigate the profession of sociology.

I am grateful for the support and investment this project has received from Mick Gusinde-Duffy, David Brunsma, and David Embrick at the University of Georgia Press.

My family has also supported me throughout this endeavor. My greatest appreciation goes to my partner, Julie Krueger. She has been supportive in more ways than I can say, but I am most grateful for her encouragement to keep a healthy work-life balance, especially during the emotionally challenging data collection phase. Lucy Schneider and Charles Krueger also deserve credit for their patience and for the sacrifices they made so that I could pursue this project.

Last but certainly not least, I am deeply appreciative of the community of volunteers who dedicate their time and resources to serving St. Louis's unhoused population. This book is not only about them but for them. It is no easy thing to welcome an outsider to study your thoughts, feelings, and interactions. Yet the volunteers who participated in this study almost always made me feel like a welcome and full participant in their work. This book's critical perspective on volunteer homeless services should not be mistaken for a lack of appreciation for volunteers who were open, honest, and committed to visions of a healthier and more supportive community. I hope that those doing the work will see that this book has been written with the same intention.

So while my name appears on the cover page, this project would not have been possible without all of you. Thank you.

Serving the Street

"Race Plays a Role in Anything That Happens, Especially in St. Louis"

Excerpt of an Interview with Mama Germaine Black, Middle-Class Volunteer with Fam in the Streets May 29, 2018

Race plays a part in just about everything we do in America, as far as human beings. Until we can get that ugly infection out the roots, yeah.

Homelessness—a lot of people used to live—you know where they building NGA [the National Geospatial-Intelligence Agency] now? A lot of people used to live there, in that community. They got eminent domained out. Plus, the street they building the hospital. Those were some housing projects . . . the houses. I think that was the Pruitt-Igoe. One time, I don't remember which one it was, Pruitt or Igoe, because it was two separate things, and one was Black and one was white.

Race plays a role in anything that happens, especially in St. Louis. I've never been in such an openly racist society. . . . I lived all over the country. I lived all over. I was like, "I ain't never seen nothing like this." But it is. It's real.

Questioning Community Service and Allyship

On the cold evening of February 10, 2018, I found myself weaving between downtown St. Louis, Missouri, and the city's infamously segregated Black North Side. I was sitting in the passenger seat of a small black Fiat with Fran, a white social worker, volunteer, and founder of Citywide Outreach; we were searching for anyone who "looks homeless." The goal was simple: get those without housing to shelter for the night. When in downtown, we peered into covered bus stops, looking for anyone who did not seem to fit into the surrounding scene of hip bars and restaurants. We checked popular congregation sites, including steam grates, fast food restaurant lobbies, parks, and social service centers. On the North Side, we circled crumbling red brick buildings and peered into any nook that might offer shelter from the wind. As we cruised around the city, conversation with Fran varied. She was quick to laugh, and the two of us exchanged funny stories and small talk. She also gave me a history lesson on homelessness and welfare in the United States—unprompted and from memory. When I asked what she knew about the locally famous Merfred graffiti, she responded with a hint of pride in her voice that she knew the artist. She explained that the artist sought to provide community members with something that they could enjoy together and that would counteract perceived group differences. Fran thought that he was a "sweet, sweet man" but doubted that he understood the "depth of racism" in the United States—or that she understood it either. She later said that she hoped to establish a coordinated network of services available across the city. Fran was incredibly thoughtful, caring, and dedicated to providing relief, even if only temporary, to people experiencing homelessness in the city she called home.

So as we drove along, passing the time through conversation, we kept our eyes peeled. If either of us spotted someone in potential need, we would immediately stop our conversation, she would whip her "tin-can car" into a U-turn, and we would park or roll down a window to ask about that person's housing arrangements for the evening. When she engaged people, whether or not she knew them, the tone in her voice was soft, communicating that she cared. It was clear to me—and, I assume, to those she approached on the street—that she was there to help.

Like many other contemporary U.S. cities, St. Louis has struggled to cope with a large unhoused population. In 2017, the year I started fieldwork in earnest, the annual point-in-time count conducted by the U.S. Department of Housing and Urban Development (HUD), which is known to undercount the number of people experiencing homelessness (Smith and Castañeda-Tinoco 2019; National Law Center on Homelessness and Poverty 2017), recorded 1,798 people experiencing homelessness in St. Louis City and St. Louis County on a single night in January.[1] Seventy-seven percent of those counted were Black

FIGURE 1. Smoke stains discolor the rear exterior of a disused public building between downtown and North City, May 29, 2021. Unhoused men frequently gathered, claimed space, and slept at this otherwise abandoned site, and a number of the outreach groups regularly stopped here. The chain link fence was periodically repaired, but those seeking shelter would soon cut the fencing or push it aside. The sign to the left reads, "City of St. Louis. No Loitering. ORD 61415." © Matthew Jerome Schneider.

(HUD 2017a,b). Homelessness has subsequently remained a persistent problem for St. Louis: the 2019 count found 1,518 people (three-quarters of them Black) experiencing homelessness (HUD 2019a,b), while the 2022 count found similar numbers—1,518 people experiencing homelessness, 72 percent of whom identified as Black (HUD 2022b,a). Nevertheless, Missouri enacted a 2022 law banning people from sleeping on state-owned property, giving the state attorney general the power to sue local governments that fail to enforce the ban, and emphasizing short-term housing rather than long-term or transitional shelters (Erickson 2022; Oladipo 2023). The city's "progressive" mayor, Tishaura Jones, who was in office from April 2021 to April 2025, and her government created controversy with their treatment of the unhoused population, which included "sweeps" involving the eviction and bulldozing of encampments near city hall and on the riverfront (Huguelet 2023; Krull 2023; Maxwell 2023).

Public and media interest in homelessness has waned since the 1980s but has not totally vanished (B. A. Lee, Tyler, and Wright 2010). U.S. news organizations fairly frequently cover homelessness as a social issue. Many churches and volunteer organizations mobilize to provide meals and nonperishable food items for the "most vulnerable among us" during the holiday season. Many city dwellers and business owners complain about the visibility of homelessness in their towns and cities. Others sympathetically nod or scrounge through their pockets for change as they pass by panhandlers. Still others have taken it upon themselves to respond to what they see as the failure of city governments.

Although I grew up in the St. Louis metropolitan area, I was well into graduate school before I took a real interest in the city's volunteer scene. Eventually, though, volunteer homeless service became a regular activity for me. Specifically, I began working with an Episcopalian service house on an occasional basis in the spring of 2016, and over the course of near-daily ethnographic research between August 2017 and August 2018, I worked with and alongside five grassroots homeless service organizations. Through this work, I met dozens of well-intentioned volunteers committed to meeting the needs of their "friends on the street." While Fran sticks out in my mind as exceptionally kind and civically minded, the other volunteers I met were also consistently willing to sacrifice their free time, money, possessions, and arguably safety to respond to the pressing problem of homelessness in their city. How do volunteers interpret, explain, and respond to this problem? What pushes (or pulls) these volunteers toward this sort of service? For those who participated regularly and invested their own resources, what inspires such dedication?

In many (but not all) ways, volunteers had a deeply structural understanding of homelessness. Among the service groups I observed, it was common to hear volunteers complain about the lack of city resources available to people experiencing homelessness, police treatment of people experiencing homelessness, and the closing of the New Life Evangelistic Center, a service center that, among other things, offered overnight shelter. Recognizing the failure of city and county governments to provide adequate human services and shelter in the St. Louis metropolitan area, a number of grassroots service groups have taken to the streets in an effort to combat the problem.

It is not difficult to understand the appeal of "homeless outreach." On my first night volunteering with Fellowship Outreach, September 7, 2017, I found myself in awe. Having grown up in the St. Louis area and having designed a dissertation research project about volunteer services, I knew about homelessness in the city. Still, that had not prepared me for that first outreach experience. As I rounded out my fieldnotes the following day, I added, "I felt like I was exposed to a new world last night, to a strange world that I knew existed, but never fully experienced, despite being intertwined with or existing just beyond the same spaces I've used my entire life." As I explored and engaged with these spaces with fresh eyes, I felt a sense of excitement and a certain wholesomeness. I spent most of that first night fixated on the casual and friendly interactions I observed between volunteers and people experiencing homelessness. It seemed important at the time that I make note of Albert, a man experiencing homelessness who participated in outreach activities as member of the group, of the friendly banter around an East Side bonfire with the St. Louis skyline looming just to the west, and of the discussion among volunteers about opportunities for their "friends," ranging from jobs to showers.

Beyond this, it also became clear that some volunteers engaged with this work because homelessness represented injustice. In a country as rich and prosperous as the United States, how can some people lack regular access to shelter? How can St. Louis have empty houses and apartments spread across the city, some falling into disrepair from disuse, *and* host hundreds of people "sleeping rough" (sleeping outdoors without cover)—in tents, in pavilions, and tucked beneath interstate exit ramps? And how does one explain the overrepresentation of Black men subjected to these conditions? Indeed, many volunteers understood their work as a form of racial justice activism and/or allyship.

And, of course, volunteer response to these problems is important. The volunteers with whom I worked were caring and empathetic people who not only recognized a problem but also sought to do something about it. Against this backdrop, however, I began to notice a number of parallel patterns that made me question whether volunteer homeless services were as effective as we might like to believe. Yes, there was a friendliness with all the groups I observed. And yes, these groups provided invaluable resources to dozens of people on a regular basis. Still, the picture was more complicated than might be noticed at first glance.

Through grassroots homeless service provision, I also witnessed structures of inequality being reproduced. Specifically, a tension exists between volunteering and privilege. The unifying thread of whiteness—a thread that runs through time and place—is its ability to protect its position atop the racial hierarchy, thereby disproportionately consuming social, political, and economic resources (Hughey 2014; Omi and Winant 1994; Wellman 1993). While individual whites may not always deliberately or even consciously engage in this process, the four-hundred-year history of European settlement in North America clearly shows the process at work (Feagin 2013; Omi and Winant 1994). Other forms of privilege, including but not limited to class and gender privilege, are protected through similar processes and intertwine with processes of racism to help prop up white supremacist society. So then, how does one make sense of the fact that the core of formal volunteering, an activity generally conceived in altruistic terms, is disproportionately composed of people who are white, middle class, and college educated (Foster-Bey 2008; Y. Lee and Brudney 2009; Pho 2008)? If the goal of voluntary service is to help, how is this intention realized when privilege seems to be a common and central feature of volunteer status? Is it possible that volunteer intentions are interrupted or shaped by processes of racialization and exclusion?

I am tempted to suggest that the answer is Yes, of course. Structural position (race, class, housing status, and the like) is of great importance in informing volunteer perception of and interaction in urban spaces. This book interrogates how racial ideologies influence the way volunteers navigate and act within spaces filled with homeless Others and Otherized urban space. This perception spurs action and conversation that sometimes reproduces problematic cultural ideas about choice, difference, and inequality.

However, a more appropriate answer might be Yes, and . . . As an increasing number of Americans openly engage with and contemplate the importance of race and whiteness, this study makes an important intervention. By critically examining the role and actions of well-meaning, privileged volunteers, this book grapples with how to respond to and cope with the uneven social landscape that even social-justice-oriented volunteers fail to consider. While racism is often framed as a product of self- or group interest (Berg 2015; Sidanius and Pratto 1999), volunteers interested in undermining systems of inequality might also represent an opportunity to undermine white-supremacist society. Although significant and common obstacles to antiracist service remain in place, particularly for majority-white volunteer groups interacting with predominantly nonwhite service populations, the ultimate purpose of this book is to understand (1) what these obstacles are, (2) how volunteers respond to these obstacles, and (3) how volunteers can more appropriately engage with the communities they seek to help.

Scope of the Book

This book explores three interlocking questions. First, much time and effort has been spent developing a sociology of whiteness, and theories of color-blind racism have been profoundly influential in the field of racial and ethnic studies. However, going forward, scholars must move beyond fixation with white identities and ideologies. While understanding them within any given context is important, studies often neglect to connect ideologies to the racialized social system that produced them. According to sociologists Matthew W. Hughey, David Embrick, and Ashley "Woody" Doane (2015), the next step is to identify and understand the mechanisms of racial inequality—that is, "the constellation of properties and actions of whites and activities that are organized to regularly bring about a particular type of outcome" (1350). Hughey, Embrick, and Doane refer specifically to color-blind ideology, but the point can also be applied to the study of those with salient white identities (e.g., white antiracists), their adjoining ideologies (e.g., pro-diversity, social justice), and the contexts that produce them. How do whites maintain their privileged social status in almost any setting? What actions—even actions carried out with the intent of undermining or relieving social and racial inequalities—construct and reinforce the racialized social system in which they exist?

Second, voluntary labor is widely practiced throughout the United States, with more than sixty-two million Americans engaged in some form of volunteering (U.S. Department of Labor, Bureau of Labor Statistics 2016). The variety of volunteer activities that exist is wide ranging, with many services aiming to provide for marginalized or "needy" populations/communities. Indeed, volunteers are often crucial in meeting the needs of many marginalized groups. Yet little work has focused on the practice of volunteering (J. Wilson 2012). In particular, this book asks how the practice of volunteering is affected by social positioning. Put differently, how do race, housing status, and class inform service provision and interactions?

Third, much of the work on the stigmatization of the poor takes the poor themselves and/or legal institutions as central objects of analysis (e.g., Beckett and Herbert 2010; Duneier 1999; Herring 2019; Reutter et al. 2009; Wasserman and Clair 2010). These studies often seek to highlight how inequality is reproduced through stigma or institutional power (Gowan 2010; Lyon-Callo 2015; Wacquant 2002; Wasserman and Clair 2010). Because these studies place the volunteer and the service provider either on the periphery of or outside the field of study, full understanding of the context and the process of stigmatization has yet to be apprehended. A tension exists among volunteers and service providers as the groups are, on the one hand, attempting to engage in work popularly viewed as altruistic (Snyder and Omoto 2008) while, on the other hand, protecting privileged statuses (e.g., middle-class, college-educated, and white)—even if unwittingly (Hughey 2014) or despite stated intentions to the contrary (Schneider 2018). In what ways do volunteers work against social problems like homelessness and racial inequality? In what ways, if any, do volunteers produce and/or reproduce social inequality?

Why Grassroots Homeless Services in St. Louis?

Although St. Louis is often referred to as the Gateway to the West, it has historically been a destination in its own right. Since its founding as a French trading post in the mid-eighteenth century, the city has been a destination for European immigrants from Germany and Ireland and Black migrants from the South, has hosted the World's Fair, and at one point was even considered to replace Washington, D.C., as the U.S. capital (Johnson 2021). Indeed, for much of the twentieth century, St. Louis was a booming metropolis and America's fourth-largest city. Now however, the boom days are a memory. In 1950, the population of St. Louis was about 850,000, and about half of the metropolitan area lived within the city limits. By the 2000 census, the city's population had dropped below 350,000 and accounted for only 13 percent of the metropolitan area's total (Gordon 2008). Population decline continues, with the 2010 census counting 319,294 people, and the 2020 census counting 301,578 people living in St. Louis City (U.S. Census Bureau 2020). Out-migration has been normal for U.S. industrial cities since the 1950s, but St. Louis finds itself in rare company with Buffalo, Cleveland, Detroit, and Pittsburgh as the only cities to have lost more than half of their population (Hollander et al. 2009). Sitting immediately across the Mississippi River, East St. Louis, Illinois, has experienced sustained economic and population decline as well, with Justin Hollander and colleagues (2009, 230) calling the city "a poster child for shrinking cities" because of its crime record, large unemployed labor force, and struggling school system (see also Gordon 2008; Reardon 2000).

In addition to economic instability, the city has experienced substantial racial strife. St. Louis City is about half white (46.7 percent) and half Black (45.6 percent) (U.S. Census Bureau 2020), but the region remains heavily segregated, with North and East St. Louis housing mostly Black residents and the southern and western suburbs housing mostly white residents. Of course, racial tension in St. Louis predates the end of World War II (e.g., *Dred Scott v. Sandford*, the 1917

FIGURE 2. Downtown St. Louis as seen from the east bank of the
Mississippi River, February 2, 2018. © Matthew Jerome Schneider.

East St. Louis Race Riots, Bleeding Kansas), but the current demographic map
was formed during the era of white flight (Gordon 2008; Heathcott and Murphy
2016; Johnson 2021). And while some parts of the metropolitan area are relatively
affluent, John E. Farley (1991; 1995; 2005) argues that the continued segregation is
first and foremost an issue of race(ism), not class. According to Farley (2005), so-
cioeconomic status explains only between 15 and 35 percent of Black-white housing segregation in the metropolitan area. In his view, housing segregation is better
explained by white preference for predominantly white communities and by the
practice of steering both white and Black families to view and buy houses in racially homogenous neighborhoods.

The tension has not dissipated with time. More recently, the St. Louis area has
been pushed into the national spotlight for problems with racism and police violence. Most notably, weeks of protest followed the August 2014 police shooting of
an unarmed Black teenager, Michael Brown, in Ferguson, Missouri, just a few minutes north of St. Louis. When officials announced that Darren Wilson, the white
officer who killed Brown, would not be charged, further protest erupted (Lockhart 2019). While newspapers generally produced a narrative that was sympathetic
to the protests and many observers responded to Brown's death by calling for police reform (Elmasry and el-Nawawy 2017; Kochel 2015), others fixated on protesters' disruption, crimes, looting, arson, and potential divisiveness (Kochel 2015).

In addition, in September 2017, during my time in the field, mass protests occurred after a white police officer, Jason Stockley, was acquitted of first-degree

murder in the 2011 shooting of Anthony Lamar Smith, a Black man. Stockley and his partner, Brian Bianchi, reportedly suspected Smith of engaging in an illegal drug transaction (Dakin and Karimi 2017). Racial justice protests do not occur only following major events, and race and racism remain salient in the minds of many St. Louisans. In fact, many of this study's participants reported belonging to antiracist and activist organizations. Many openly color-conscious volunteers cited racial injustice as the impetus for their homeless outreach or saw racial justice work as an important component of their volunteer work.

In some ways, St. Louis is exceptional. For a period following Brown's murder, the area was the epicenter of the Black Lives Matter movement. Since at least that time, conversation about race and racism has taken a form that is more public and open than is seen in other parts of the country. In other ways, though, St. Louis represents a typical case. While St. Louis has been impacted more dramatically by industrial decline and white flight than have most cities, these processes can be observed in urban centers across the United States. Thus, I viewed St. Louis as an ideal field site that would offer lessons and insights likely to be observed outside the St. Louis metro region (Schofield 2002). Specifically, with an interest in un-

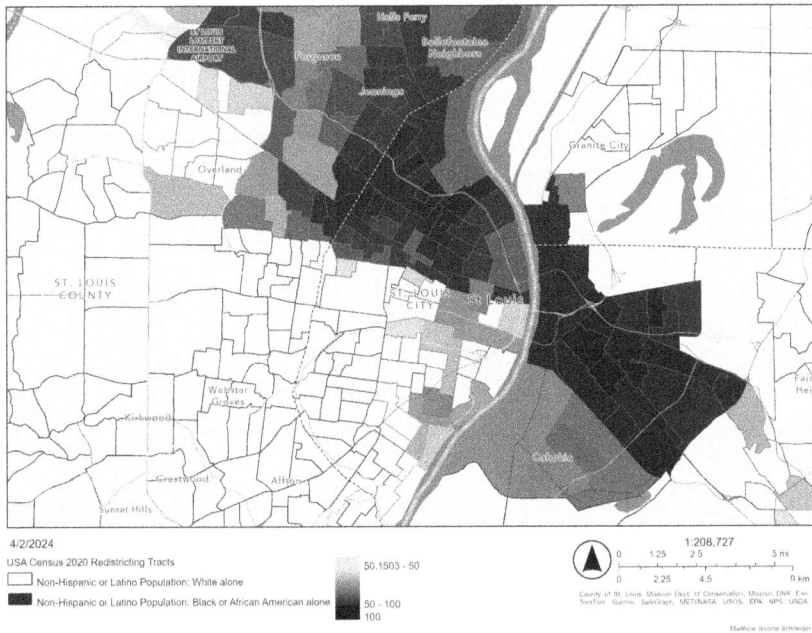

FIGURE 3. Map showing racial segregation by census tract in the St. Louis Metropolitan Area. Data from the 2020 U.S. Census. © Matthew Jerome Schneider.

derstanding service relationships, privilege, and especially racial privilege, I turned to St. Louis's robust grassroots homeless services scene.

According to the volunteers I asked, people experiencing homelessness could be identified by the clothes they wear, how they act, or the bags they carry. Few if any volunteers would suggest that they stop more frequently for Black pedestrians, and some even doubt that the unhoused population is disproportionately Black. The data suggest otherwise. Despite the limitations of the annual point-in-time count (Smith and Castañeda-Tinoco 2019; National Law Center on Homelessness and Poverty 2017), it is useful for understanding the general demographics of the unhoused population, especially when looking specifically at who is being temporarily sheltered on the night of the count. Whereas counts have consistently shown that about three-quarters of the unhoused population is Black, African Americans comprise only 45.9 percent of the total population in the city and 24.9 percent of the county's population (U.S. Census Bureau 2019b,a). Using data from the American Community Survey, the City of St. Louis's website estimates that Black residents are nearly four times more likely to be homeless than are white residents ("Homelessness" n.d.).

"Homelessness" can refer to a wide range of experiences. In this study, observation was generally of people who lived precariously without access to permanent housing, frequently spending their nights in abandoned buildings or tents, on the street or ground, or in a shelter bed. The exceptions were people living at Mercy House, which not only served people living precariously but also housed a small number of women, families, and transgender people for comparatively long periods of time (usually a few months). Most of the people experiencing homelessness with whom I interacted were Black men of varying ages. St. Louis's geography of homelessness has a segregated nature. It was common to see large congregations of Black men spread throughout the city, especially in the downtown area near social service centers. But volunteer groups also knew of camps that were less obvious or totally hidden to the average passerby. Most of these camps were small—as few as one to three people—and most of the camp residents were white. These camps were well served by a number of volunteer groups, including Right Choice and Fellowship.

Homelessness in St. Louis does not command the academic or popular attention attracted by large urban centers such as Los Angeles, San Francisco, Seattle, and New York (e.g., Beckett and Herbert 2010; Duneier 1999; Gowan 2010; Herring 2019; Stuart 2016). Similarly, the problem of rural homelessness rightfully merits increased attention (e.g., Lawrence 1995; Meehan 2019; Wiltz 2015). But homelessness in St. Louis and other smaller, declining industrial cities is also important to consider. Even if homelessness in smaller, more affordable cities lacks the scale or visibility of homelessness in high-cost-of-living coastal cities, home-lessness is not unique to these places. And because homelessness is an expensive problem to address, smaller cities may not be willing or able to dedicate the nec-essary financial resources to productive solutions. In turn, outreach and volunteer activities may be of greater significance in these contexts (Ashwood et al. 2019).

Methods

I collected data through participant observation and semistructured interviews. The volunteer groups that participated in the project provided temporary or emergency shelter; transportation to shelter; and food, blankets, tents and/or other supplies to people experiencing homelessness. The groups operated solely on voluntary labor, and the members of most groups were predominantly white, middle class, and college educated. The data collected consequently reflect this demographic makeup. Preliminary research was conducted in the spring of 2016, and primary data collection was conducted between August 2017 and Au-gust 2018. The six participating groups fall into three categories: nondenomi-national Christian organizations, secular/activist organizations, and Catholic/ Episcopalian service houses. I conducted forty-five semistructured interviews with forty-three group volunteers.[2] Interviews focused on volunteer interactions and the problem of homelessness. More than 250 hours of participant observa-tion brought me into contact with countless other volunteers, service groups, and people experiencing homelessness, and I recorded these encounters in my field notes. Most of the photographs were taken in May and June 2021 as part of a separate project and are included to provide readers with a better understand-ing of the built environment volunteers were navigating.

To protect participant confidentiality, all people are referred to by pseud-onyms, as are organizations and volunteer groups, and faces in photographs have been obscured. Moreover, in light of the social and spatial tensions between the unhoused, law enforcement, city governments, business owners, pedestrians, and other social actors, common gathering spots, encampments, places of stay, and other geographic locations are described only in vague terms. However, sociospa-tial boundaries are important to understanding volunteering in context. For ex-ample, North St. Louis and East St. Louis have been subjects of numerous racist historical projects that have resulted in concentrated poverty, crumbling infra-structure, and intense racial segregation. Recognizing the importance of this leg-acy, references to large areas of the city are included, though specific neighbor-hoods are not.

The six groups with whom I worked were chosen based on their accessibility. I found two groups online, and they responded when I reached out. I added three others through mutual contacts established after I began my fieldwork. A friend facilitated my involvement with the sixth organization.

To emphasize local meanings and context, I approached the project via the grounded theory method (Corbin and Strauss 2008). I conducted background research before beginning my fieldwork, and because I expected that the project's findings would relate to race, whiteness, and urban space, my interview questions were designed to explore such issues. I wrote memos during the course of my fieldwork but did not transcribe interviews or conduct data analysis until I had concluded my fieldwork. Data were coded first for general themes and then again line by line. Quotations and excerpts from field notes presented in this volume represent common themes/patterns that emerged (Corbin and Strauss 2008; Miles and Huberman 1984; Weiss 1994). Not all participant voices are quoted in this book, while some—people with whom I spent more time (Paul, Gabriela, and Peter), prominent actors who were sources of guidance for other volunteers (Fran, Peter, John), and people who were especially insightful (Barbara, Paul, René)—appear multiple times.

Throughout the data-collection process, I tried to remain cognizant of my social statuses and how my status might affect the data gathered (Heyl 2001). This was a constant process, although I am certain that I could not account for all the ways my status as a researcher and housed white cisgender man impacted data collection. Nevertheless, I am aware that my statuses and performance affected my interactions and data collection. First, my entry into the field was through the volunteer groups, and people experiencing homelessness generally interacted with me as they would any other white, middle-class volunteer. Generally, they were friendly and open, but if I tried to press beyond small talk to ask about volunteer groups, I was usually met with skepticism. Although this was less than ideal (Goffman 1989), there was also great benefit to working side by side with the volunteers. Many of the groups treated me as a full participant despite knowing that I was also conducting research on their group. I do not believe that my status negatively impacted the quality of data when interacting with groups of predominantly white, middle-class volunteers. Instead, my similarities to them and my regular participation in group activities seemed to grant me an insider status, trust, and rapport (Greene 2014). The many hours I spent traversing the city with members of these groups, listening to their ideas and opinions, and making polite conversation certainly cemented my position within the groups and provided them with a positive opinion of me. Likewise, I enjoyed my time with many of these groups and regularly expressed my genuine appreciation for them. I believe this contributed to rich data collection, especially when interviewees shared information with me under the impression that I would share similar or complementary viewpoints, which, in the case of the explicitly color-conscious volunteers, was usually true (Goffman 1989; Greene 2014; Sherry 2008).

My relationship to these volunteers has also colored my opinion of them and by extension the way I have interpreted, analyzed, and framed the data. I have tried to simultaneously acknowledge the tangible impacts of the services they provide, appreciate their desire to respond to pressing community problems, and assess their efforts with a critical eye.

The Volunteer Groups

Homeless outreach and other forms of volunteering are incredibly popular in St. Louis. As a participant-observer, I worked alongside volunteers from the six sampled organizations, but many similar groups existed. During the course of fieldwork, I became aware of at least six other grassroots outreach organizations, and since fieldwork concluded, I have learned that at least three more groups have started or splintered off from parent groups. During the winter months, local news outlets often produce a flurry of stories about the work of these homeless service groups and profile individual volunteers.

Four of the groups with which I worked had an overt religious character, and at some point in the groups' histories, all four had been formally affiliated with a church or religious organization. The other two groups I observed were officially secular. Prayer was not a regular part of either group's outreach, but group prayer did happen on (very rare) occasions, and a number of group members credited their faith for spurring their participation in these secular organizations. As the literature on volunteering would have predicted (Foster-Bey 2008), a large majority of the volunteers I met and interacted with were white, although Fam in the Streets was fairly diverse and Citywide Outreach relied heavily on partnering with emergency shelters located in Black churches spread across the city's North Side.

Two of the six groups I observed, Fellowship Outreach and Right Choice Ministry and Outreach, included religious practice as a part of their service. Fellowship Outreach was originally part of a larger evangelistic center, but the group continued to conduct outreach on a year-round, weekly basis after the center closed. At the time of my observation, members of Fellowship Outreach had been providing their "homeless friends" with sodas, snacks, meals, clothing, batteries, tents, and other supplies for about five years. Right Choice was composed primarily of members of a nondenominational congregation and provided similar outreach services. Both relied heavily on prayer, and Right Choice leaders were known to regularly consider whether they were doing enough to promote God's Word as a part of their outreach missions. This rarely came up as an issue for members of Fellowship, however.[3] Members of these groups tended to espouse ideologies that emphasized individualism, hard work, and color blindness. Although the degree to which volunteers were willing to acknowledge the continued importance of race and racism in American society varied, Eduardo Bonilla-Silva's (2010) four frames of color-blind racism, especially abstract liberalism, minimization of racism, and cultural racism, were commonly deployed during volunteer interviews. Michael O. Emerson and Christian Smith (2000) detail the association between the evangelicalism, individualism, and color blindness. Although neither Fellowship nor Right Choice were officially evangelical organizations, Protestant notions of the individual and achievement (Berger 1990; Weber 2011) were well represented and paired well with the groups' color-blind disposition.

Four groups—Citywide Outreach, Mercy House, Service House, and Fam in the Streets—made a conscious effort to operate out of social and racial justice frameworks or identified as progressive activists and viewed their volunteer activities as an enactment of their activism. Citywide's primary focus was a network of pop-up shelters on nights when the temperature was forecasted to drop below twenty degrees Fahrenheit (or below twenty-five degrees with precipitation) and to transporting unhoused individuals to these shelters. Fam in the Streets often joined Citywide in this mission and gained limited local fame for their "caravan of love" that traveled around the city on Thursday nights serving hot meals to people experiencing homelessness. Mercy House was a Catholic Worker house and shelter located on the predominantly Black North Side that also offered free weekend breakfasts, free sandwiches for anyone who came to the door, and free donated clothing. Service House, my site for preliminary data collection, was a group of young Episcopalian adults who had committed themselves to a year of service. They lived in an intentional community on the North Side and spent their days serving at local nonprofits, three of which directly or indirectly provided services to people experiencing homelessness.

In contrast to the first two groups, members of these groups tended to be explicitly color-conscious. While members of the other two groups usually needed to be asked how they felt about race and racism in St. Louis, these volunteers generally broached the subject as they analyzed poverty and homelessness. Although they might not have used the same language as scholars of race and racism, they articulated race as a system of oppression. Thus, they viewed racism not just as individual prejudice but also as a combination of practices and ideologies that could be embedded in institutions such as the city government, the criminal legal system, and the educational system.

Plan of the Book

Chapter 1 offers a more thorough introduction to common narratives that frame homelessness and volunteer response to it. Building from Teresa Gowan's (2010) concepts of sin-talk, sick-talk, and system-talk, the chapter explores how volunteers went through a process of norming. Responding to their group's favored discourse, volunteers found a group, learned to fit in, and stayed in. These common forms of discourse took local form but emerged from a wider cultural conversation about poverty in the United States and worked in tandem with volunteers' understandings of race.

Chapter 2 explores the beliefs, attitudes, and practices of service groups with color-blind attitudes. Both groups featured in this chapter, Right Choice and Fellowship, were Protestant Christian organizations that focused on direct relief in the form of handouts and interpersonal connection. Beyond their emphasis on charity and their religious orientations, these groups were also characterized by their reliance on individualistic explanations of homelessness. They relied on common cultural narratives such as homelessness as choice or as the consequence of addiction, individual failure, or laziness to justify their individual-oriented service practices, which seemed to favor interaction with white people experiencing homelessness. By relying on such narratives, volunteers sidestepped the continued importance of race (Gallagher 2003) even as they maintained friendlier relationships with whites experiencing homelessness.

Chapter 3 focuses on explicitly color-conscious volunteers as a means of highlighting the limits of service and allyship when conducted without critically examining volunteers' positions. Although they conceptualized their work to go beyond charity and toward social and racial justice, even the most color-conscious volunteers, many of whom spoke unprompted about structural inequality and systemic racism, struggled to see how *their* race was important in daily life. When asked how their race might inform their interactions with people of color experiencing homelessness, white, color-conscious volunteers were usually quick to admit that it must play a role but were also unable to say exactly how it did so or provide examples. This inability to speak about interracial interactions despite much practice with it highlights the pervasive power and privilege embedded in the taken-for-granted nature of whiteness (Doane 1997; P. McIntosh 1989). Despite displaying strong knowledge of structural racism and/or antiracism literature, their whiteness remained invisible to them.

Chapter 4 examines how volunteer understandings of homelessness, race, and urban space impact motivation, practice, and the reproduction of marginality. The privileges and power associated with volunteers' statuses, especially as white and middle-class, shape perception of, access to, and interaction in nonwhite urban spaces. Again, volunteer understandings of homelessness were intimately intertwined with notions of Blackness and urban space (Kirschenman and Neckerman 1991). In particular, this chapter interrogates volunteers' desire to explore Otherness and the touristic nature of their work. And while the slum/poverty tourism literature more frequently problematizes international tourism and volunteering (e.g., Frenzel 2015; Steinbrink 2012), I repeatedly observed volunteers, both Black and white, both color-blind and color-conscious, profess interest in "urban decay" and take photos with such frequency that one volunteer jokingly asked another volunteer if she "ever feel[s] like a Japanese tourist." In these moments, volunteers sought to explore their home city in a way few others of their class status would, in the process emphasizing the difference between themselves and those "on the street."

Having established the existence of the "volunteer gaze," this chapter then explores how that gaze racializes poverty and urban space. Color-blind volunteers (and some color-conscious volunteers), for example, responded to and reproduced stereotypes about the danger of Black neighborhoods and Black men experiencing homelessness. These stereotypes often influenced volunteers' movements around the city—for example, when volunteers elected to avoid the North Side after dark in favor of mostly white homeless camps. Explicitly color-conscious volunteers often framed their work as an opportunity to consume an "authentic" Black Otherness. For these groups, the intersection of Blackness and poverty promised a culturally rich if not novel encounter with marginality. In both cases, volunteers cast their gazes on racialized Others and reified homogenizing and damaging narratives about the people they sought to help.

Finally, the conclusion considers the implications of these findings for future volunteer practice. Although volunteers who have privileged statuses pose significant challenges to providing socially just solutions to homelessness, throwing the baby out with the bathwater might be ill-advised. These volunteers have recognized a real problem in their community and sought to do something about it in the face of the city's failure. Their actions are both commendable and require critical interrogation. Alongside the need for greater reflexivity even among well-intentioned, social-justice-oriented volunteers lies the need for intergroup coalitions and collective action. Furthermore, given the strong pattern of group norming that I observed, altering conversations about race, poverty, and homelessness within groups may prove useful in adjusting service expectations and practices.

CHAPTER 1

"Really Psychotic"

Excerpt of Fieldnotes from Citywide Outreach
December 28, 2017

Citywide Outreach is a group of volunteers who do the bulk of their work in the winter months. During these months, the group works with a number of local churches to open as emergency shelters when the temperature drops below twenty degrees Fahrenheit or below twenty-five degrees if there is precipitation.[1] On these nights, the group meets at a South City coffeehouse owned and operated by one of the group's more involved members. From there, volunteers pair up and spread across the city in search of people in need of blankets, stocking caps, gloves, handwarmers, snacks, and/or transportation to emergency shelters. On these cold nights, the coffeehouse serves another purpose: it is a place for volunteers to iron out their understandings of the mission as well as of homelessness. Each new attendee is paired with a veteran volunteer, and they receive and sign a set of rules.[2] But the coffeehouse is also a setting in which volunteers can meet and trade stories from the field. On this particular evening, group members took time to express some of their recent frustrations while volunteering.

Vincent, a white man in his early forties, was the most animated in his complaints. He told other volunteers, including me, that he had been close to getting a group of four people experiencing homelessness to go in for shelter and a meal—as he put it, trying to convince "one A-hole to let three other A-holes" go in for the night. The four people wanted to stick together, but one didn't want to spend the night in a shelter. Vincent believed that he would have succeeded except that someone from another outreach group had recently given the group members a small amount of kerosene for their lamp. He expressed frustration over their logic and desire to stay outside: if they had agreed to come in, not only would the kerosene have lasted longer, but they would also have had "food and security." A sarcastic man with a somewhat dry sense of humor, Vincent's use of the term "A-holes" was partly rooted in his personality, but it was also rooted in his frustration. On multiple occasions, Vincent expressed to me that he really believes in what he is doing and is committed to this cause. He sees shelter as the most important thing that outreach groups can offer, and by airing his frustrations publicly, he made a case for his vision of homeless services as well as for what he imagines life to be like for those without consistent shelter.

As the meeting progressed, each volunteer was assigned a partner and told which area of the city to go to. Some experienced volunteers wanted to try to find particular people or were familiar with particular areas of the city, so assignments were made through a combination of Vincent's choice and volunteers' expressed interest. After assignments were completed, partners began moving toward the staircase so that they could collect supplies from the storage area in the basement.

Before I left with Gabriela, a white retired social worker, however, she wanted to pass on information to another white volunteer, Aaron, about a recent encounter with Miss Alberta, a Black woman experiencing homelessness about whom Gabriela routinely worried. Gabriela told Aaron to check on Miss Alberta, who would likely be bundled up under a bus stop near a downtown park and who was "really psychotic": "She really believes she might be Hillary Clinton." Like Vincent, Gabriela intended her comments to be partially humorous, but she also hoped to relay information she deemed valuable. In addition to eliciting a laugh or two, her comments spoke to her understanding of people experiencing homelessness, communicated what she felt Aaron needed to know, and expressed concern for the person. Included in this information was a subtext: Aaron should dedicate extra effort and attention to making sure Miss Alberta was accounted for and that her most obvious needs were being met.

Learning How to Serve

Meaning-Making and Volunteer Discourse about Homelessness

The academic literature has convincingly argued that homeless service provision is largely based on the belief that homelessness is "caused" by individual choices and (im)morality (Gowan 2010; Lyon-Callo 2015; Wasserman and Clair 2010; Willse 2015). It has also been suggested that interpersonal interaction with people experiencing homelessness does little to change people's opinions about approaches to homeless services (Knecht and Martinez 2009). However, the process by which service approaches are entrenched or innovated is not well discussed. As I observed interactions like those from December 28, 2017, I became increasingly aware of just how important peer interaction was to informing volunteers' thoughts, opinions, and actions. Volunteers participated in what symbolic interaction theorists such as Herbert Blumer (1969) might call meaning-making. Through this process, volunteers are not only influenced by social structure (i.e., culture and institutions) but also help undermine and/or reproduce social structure as they interpret and interact with their surroundings.

Interactions during the course of service provide volunteers with an opportunity to work out their understandings of race, poverty, homelessness, urban space, and service provision. While this process would include interactions with people experiencing homelessness, I did not interpret these interactions as the most influential for volunteer understanding. More important than observation of poverty and the spaces they encountered were their conversations with people who have (1) a similar social position to their own and (2) similar "evidence" on which to draw as they try to make sense of the social world and/or support their worldview.

In particular, volunteer groups reproduced discourses about the immorality of homelessness, systemic oppression of the poor, and homelessness as a product of disease, sickness, and/or addiction—what sociologist Teresa Gowan (2010, 27) calls "sin-talk," "system-talk," and "sick-talk." Based on these within-group conversations, volunteers' ideas about inequality and mobility are modified and/or entrenched. In other words, volunteering, especially in group settings, serves as a process of meaning-making. Ultimately, groups seemed to attract volunteers who were of similar position and perspective, engaged in regular discourse to iron out competing differences, and approached their service work with the same or similar goals.

Meaning-Making

Understanding the world from a symbolic interactionist (si) perspective equates to understanding the process of meaning-making. The si perspective has perhaps best been articulated by George Herbert Mead and Herbert Blumer. For Mead (1962), the social world is constructed and reconstructed through shared understanding of symbols exchanged between socialized members of society. Because people are subject to this process, individuals are able to see their socialized selves, their "mes," as objects and are able to anticipate the expectations of those around them—what Mead refers to as the generalized other. Meanwhile, the actions of others, including gestures, language, facial expressions, and the like, serve as symbols to be continuously interpreted, reinforced, and negotiated. Similarly, Blumer (1969) outlines the si approach in three parts: "Human beings act toward things on the basis of meanings that things have for them," "the meaning of such things is derived from, or arises out of, the social interaction that one has with one's fellows," and "these meanings are handled in, and modified through, an interpretative process used by the person in dealing with the things he encounters" (2). Put more simply, symbolic interactionists suggest that interpreted and shared meaning are central to understanding social construction. Meaning is shared in, derived from, and altered through a process of social interaction.

Rather than seeing social structure as a rigid abstraction that determines behavior and thought, symbolic interactionism views social structure as the result of interaction of people or social groups. Symbolic interactionism moves away from structuralism by emphasizing agency, situational interaction, subjectivity, and interpretation. In any given moment (although not always), people think before they act, contemplating a response to those with whom they interact. Their responses are ultimately determined by their interpretation of others' symbolic gestures. There is no objective reality, only what is produced, reproduced, and altered through interpretation and interaction. Likewise Erving Goffman (1959; 1967) emphasizes the situational nature of interactions: "Together the participants contribute to a single over-all definition of the situation which involves not so much a real agreement as to what exists but rather a real agreement as to whose claims concerning what issues will be temporarily honored" (1967, 21).

However, the SI perspective does not dismiss the importance of social structure in favor of agency. Instead, the SI perspective is better understood as a reorientation of the structuralist perspective. Mead (1962), for example, argues that while actors' actions cannot be predicted, even by themselves (the result of a spontaneous "I") and humans are capable of choosing which action to take, action is often contained by their sense of the generalized other (the "me"). Actors are not passive but generally re-create the social conditions in which they reside. In this way, social context and social structure are important. To interpret and respond to the actions of others, Mead's actors must first be socialized in a way that allows them to understand the generalized other. Goffman's (1959) actors respond to mostly predictable and patterned expectations when on the "front stage." Even Harold Garfinkel's (1967) breaching experiments showcase the ability of nonnormative action to drastically impact the process of interpretation, meaningmaking, and response while also highlighting the boundaries of social structure.

Volunteering thus acts as a process of meaning-making (and meaning reinforcement). Interactions with other volunteers and people experiencing homelessness help inform the beliefs and actions of those participating in group activities. In particular, interactions with other volunteers cement common understandings of homelessness as sin, systemic oppression, and/or mental illness.

Understandings of Homelessness in the United States and Homeless Service Provision

There are personal, public, and social costs to homelessness. In the United States, homelessness is associated with many negative social and health outcomes: shortened lifespan; elevated risk of cancer through sun exposure, cigarette smoking, and alcoholism; and chronic medical conditions that include cardiovascular disease and tuberculosis. Psychotic and affective disorders are also fairly common (Goodman, Saxe, and Harvey 1991; Schanzer et al. 2007). These heavy health burdens lead many people who are experiencing homelessness to turn to emergency departments at a rate higher than that of the general public, even if those people receive primary care at public shelters (Ensign and Santelli 1997; Schanzer et al. 2007).

Explanations of extreme poverty vary, but popular subjects in the literature include segregated networks (Domínguez and Watkins 2003; Massey, Gross, and

Eggers 1991), structural changes (e.g., deindustrialization) (Moller et al. 2003), inadequate welfare systems (Benjaminsen and Andrade 2015; Edin and Shaefer 2015; Moller et al. 2003), and social exclusion (Newman and Massengill 2006; Zuberi 2006). Other explanations identify microlevel processes or events as reasons for homelessness (e.g., being laid off, substance abuse) (Crane et al. 2005; Main 1998; Rossi 1989). The paths to homelessness are not fixed, however, and people likely experience homelessness as a consequence of some combination of structural constraints and personal events. Structural conditions, such as high unemployment or rising housing costs, often accentuate individual circumstances such as illness, deaths of family members, and the like (Crane et al. 2005; Main 1998).

The ongoing conversation about poverty and homelessness in the United States demonstrates that the welfare state and other government institutions are not equipped to meet the needs of the poor (Benjaminsen and Andrade 2015; Moller et al. 2003) and that other social institutions (volunteer organizations, churches, local service providers, etc.) have become vital to the delivery of services to the poor (Bolger 2021; Moffitt 2015; Purser and Hennigan 2017). In addition, people experiencing poverty have been highly stigmatized by social, cultural, and political discourses about poverty (Beckett and Herbert 2010; Duneier 1999; Gowan 2010; Lyon-Callo 2000, 2015; Markowitz and Syverson 2021; Reutter et al. 2009; Wasserman and Clair 2010).

People experiencing homelessness are often framed as being responsible for their plight (Belcher and DeForge 2012; Lyon-Callo 2000; Phelan et al. 1995). And at the governmental level, homelessness is often treated as problem that can be managed through punishment. In many towns and cities, activities of daily living—urinating, sleeping, and even sitting on the sidewalk—are criminalized when conducted in public. Likewise, police, local businesses, and local residents may harass people deemed to be misusing public space (Amster 2003, 2008; Aykanian and Lee 2016; Beckett and Herbert 2010; Mitchell and Heynen 2009). Even measures that are seen as merciful and well intentioned, like "therapeutic policing," which aims to promote "moral discipline" in homeless subjects, undermines the ability/right to exist in and make use of public space (Bayat 2010; Stuart 2016). If the goal is, as some of the volunteers interviewed suggest, to discourage homelessness through punitive measures, it would be hard to view these policies as successful. Rather than quelling homelessness, they simply dislocate homelessness from desirable urban space (Beckett and Herbert 2010; Herring 2019).

Public opinion does not necessarily reflect the antihomelessness agenda pushed by the state but is also somewhat contradictory. Even as the public increasingly voices support for governmental service provision and housing-first initiatives, people also maintain interest in excluding those experiencing homelessness from desirable public space (Clifford and Piston 2017; Herring 2019; Tsai et al. 2017). Scott Clifford and Spencer Piston (2017) show that individuals can support both exclusionary homeless policy and more liberal homeless welfare policy initiatives. Furthermore, Paul Toro and colleagues (2007) find that Americans remain less compassionate and more likely to attribute homelessness to personal failings, drug and/or alcohol addition, and criminality than do people in other Western industrialized countries such as Italy, the United Kingdom, Belgium, and Germany.

Moral interpretations frame people experiencing homelessness as individuals who either have chosen to be homeless or have rejected the rules and moral underpinnings of society, thereby casting homelessness as a product of sin and individual fault—what Gowan (2010) terms sin-talk. Conversely, Gowan's concept of system-talk discourse constructs homelessness as an outcome of systemic conditions such as high unemployment rates or an inadequate welfare system. Finally, Gowan's idea of sick-talk frames the problem as resulting from (mental) illness, although the focus remains on individuals and their willingness/ability to receive treatment.

There is no shortage of academic work dedicated to studying the caring atmosphere provided by shelters (e.g., Conradson 2003; Johnsen, Cloke, and May 2005; Parr 2000) or to improving service practices (e.g., Hopper, Bassuk, and Olivet 2010; McGraw et al. 2010). However, critical studies of homelessness usually complicate the homeless service industry. At best, the industry contributes to the continued stigmatization of the unhoused. At worst, welfare institutions are tools of neoliberalism, utilized to devalue the lives of those experiencing homelessness in relation to those doing "productive work." Sociologists Jason Adam Wasserman and Jeffrey M. Clair (2010), for example, show that Christian service groups and religious institutions harbor Calvinistic notions of work and morality in a way that stigmatizes people experiencing homelessness. Somewhat similarly, Vincent Lyon-Callo (2000) draws attention to the mundane practices of service workers that discipline homeless individuals and/or reproduce homelessness as a medical condition: both individuals experiencing homelessness and service staff look to identify the "cause" of someone's homelessness, with substance abuse and/or mental illness being common diagnoses. By individualizing homelessness, discourse about homelessness as a structural outcome is deemphasized and/or discouraged (Gowan 2010; Lyon-Callo 2000). Rather than mobilizing around efforts to reduce poverty in the community because doing so would be "unrealistic," service staff devise "treatment" plans that emphasize individual solutions such as finding (typically low-wage) work, managing mental illness, and otherwise engaging in self-reform. Such plans, Lyon-Callo (2000) argues, train service recipients to blame themselves for their position.

Craig Willse (2015) adds that the social welfare industry functions as an extension of a neoliberal economy. The contemporary welfare system manages "surplus life" (i.e., people experiencing homelessness) as an extension of the economy. Local, state, and federal policies devalue human lives by producing narratives about the morality of work. In this view, "spaces of care" (e.g., shelters, resource centers) reform/discipline homeless subjects and contain people experiencing homelessness (Purser and Hennigan 2017; Willse 2015). In this light, it is hardly surprising that many people experiencing homelessness avoid utilizing services meant to "get people back on their feet" (Donley and Wright 2012; Hoffman and Coffey 2008; Lyon-Callo 2000; Wagner 1993).

Although a few studies have explored how volunteers and other service providers understand homelessness, discussion about the ways in which those ideas are shared, developed, and/or reinforced remains scant. The volunteers I interviewed spoke of finding a group that was roughly in line with their ideological viewpoint, learning to fit in, and staying fit-in. Through this process, they leaned heavily on the "expertise" of their peers and ultimately helped reproduce discourses about homelessness as sickness, sin, and/or systemic oppression.

Volunteer Socialization: Finding a Group, Fitting In, and Staying In

Volunteers had preexisting ideas about race, poverty, homelessness, and/or how to best provide service when they joined groups. However, volunteering served as a process of further socialization. Through observation of homelessness as well as interaction with peers of similar status, volunteers gained information that enabled them to revise and/or solidify their views. The process of meaning-making through volunteering started with the search for a home organization that would expose them to palatable messages about the service they hoped to perform. Mary, a white volunteer, for example, joined Service House:

> because I had a gap year. I wanted to do something that kind of went along with the social services field. That way I could test my hand at some sort of work in that area before I invested in it and found out that I hated it and was stuck with a master's [degree in social work]. And also, I wanted to do the Episcopal [group] because there are very few people my age that are Christian but also like kind of cool Christian. I had done the whole Christian thing in university. I tried to join some of those groups, but it was very much like evangelicals—super emotional,

really conservative, and not my jam. So I wanted something that was Episcopal and with people my age, which are two things that usually don't coincide.

In addition to a desire to "test [her] hand" at work in social services before committing to a master's degree in social work, Mary desired to be a part of a group that would share her worldview. She had tried joining Christian groups in the past, but because they were neither Episcopalian nor "kind of cool Christian," she did not enjoy the experience. Service House, however, seemed to offer an enjoyable experience and a progressive ideology that aligned with her own. As part of a national program that all but guaranteed that Mary would encounter people who shared her outlook, Service House would not challenge her understanding of poverty, inequality, and religion. She sought people who could affirm or develop her worldview in a way that meshed with her existing sensibilities.

When volunteers found groups with whom they clicked, the next step was to learn to how to fit into the group's mission and worldview. Whether they were new to the group or seasoned veterans, volunteers often spoke about learning from each other, particularly in reference to one or two volunteers whom they respected and who were taking the "right" approach to serving people experiencing homelessness. Not surprisingly, experienced volunteers were among the most influential. Veronica, a white volunteer who was among the most active members of Right Choice, explained that she follows the wisdom of the group's leader, John. Encountering what she saw as two competing philosophies for homeless service (relationship building and provision of physical items such as blankets, propane, food, and water), she explained that John "started the group,"

> so obviously I trust him as the leader at his word. I know he spends lots of time praying for the outreach and seeking help, talking to the pastors and other organizations. And I believe relationships are important, because if you don't have— you can have all the things in the world, and they can be taken care of, but if you don't in the end have Jesus, then all that means nothing. So I think relationships are important.

During my observation of Right Choice, this "debate" was always one-sided—everyone agreed on the need for relationships, either verbally or by nodding as others commented. Group members echoed various versions of the same idea: necessary items should be provided, but the group should be careful about how much and to whom it gave. Volunteers feared "enabling" people to be homeless for extended periods of time: giving more than the minimum might prevent people experiencing homelessness from being motivated to "change their situation." Fairly regular conversations about the issue allowed group members to stay on the same page about what homelessness meant and how to respond to it. Right Choice volunteers felt that they could skirt the issue of enabling by dedicating the bulk of their time and effort to forming and deepening relationships with people experiencing homelessness and that the provision of supplies should not play a central role in their mission. Rather than simply say why she felt relationships should be the group's priority, Veronica explained that she came to this conclusion through her respect for John's expertise.

In other cases, volunteers spoke of ongoing dialogue. Fellowship Outreach, for example, came to similar conclusions about the importance of relationships after several years and a number of leadership changes. According to Alena, a Black volunteer and Fellowship's co-leader, along with Peter,

> A lot of people are used to us just handing out the stuff. So they just want stuff, and they'll leave, but there are those people who appreciate our presence. They just want to talk. They just want to see us each week, know that somebody's coming out there to see them. Lately, we had a lot of people coming out. There's other groups that do what we do. There always have been other groups that do what we do, so yeah. It's getting back to that, and that's what Peter and I agreed that it should be at all points.

When asked why the group continued to hand out supplies, Alena responded,

> We always have, whether it was a little or a lot. So in the beginning it was a little, in the middle it was a lot, and currently it's dwindled down to a little bit. They still need stuff. Whenever it's coldest, you know, they need it. We try not to get into that mentality of being stingy with it. However, we want to be conscientious with it, because they're in survival mode, a lot of them, and they figure "if I don't get as much as I can, from as many people as I can—I won't go without." And they know that better than any of us. A lot of us who have homes and have food readily available, we don't think that way.
>
> So it's also a conduit to even open up conversation with them, even meeting them there. They expect that we'll have things, but like I said, a lot of them just— they want to see us. So both are necessary—the fellowship and the supplies.

Alena and Fellowship, like Right Choice, saw their primary mission as building relationships. Alena and Peter considered and reconsidered their group's function over several years, ultimately deciding to prioritize relationship building and using the provision of supplies and food as a means to initiate those relationships, a cost of doing business. Fellowship worked out a more moderate stance on the meanings and causes of homelessness than that of Right Choice. Alena believed that although Fellowship was "hustled" by some people experiencing homelessness who simply wanted supplies, engaging with such people was necessary to identify those who desired fellowship.

At other times, the socialization into group beliefs was more informal. Paul, a white live-in member of Mercy House, was inducted into the group as a teenager:

> We were just there from nine o'clock to like four o'clock every day for the month of January in 2012. Fran gave me my first tour of Mercy House. She is my idol/inspiration/hopefully my mentor. But I don't really know how that works. . . .
>
> We hung out. We played with the kids. We cooked a lot of lunches, which is really fun. I learned how to cook—and forgot. Forgot all of it, because I went to college and didn't cook anything for myself for like three years. But we also had a lot of downtime, so [I] read a lot of [Mercy House newsletters].[3] We watched documentaries. We even watched TV on one of the house-person's laptop computer. He had a bunch of files of episodes of *How I Met Your Mother* . . . so we would just chill upstairs and watch that sometimes. . . . I learned a lot about [the] Occupy [movement], which was happening at that time, and about the neighborhood, the North Side, Pruitt-Igoe. . . . We watched a movie about that. I was just really inspired by what they were doing, living with formerly homeless people in their home, and it just seemed really really radical and awesome.

Like Veronica, Paul respected Fran, a former member of Mercy House and the founder of Citywide. Paul also delved into the details of the socialization process, which occurred not only through formal volunteer outings but also through informal time spent together at Mercy House. In this setting, exposure to "radical" thinking took a number of forms. The Mercy House newsletter exposed Paul to writings of other house members, while the documentary presented conversations about systemic racism, housing policy, and urban planning (Birmingham 1999; Heathcott 2012). Even watching sitcoms might have fostered a sense of inclusion in life at Mercy House or spurred conversations that would not otherwise have occurred. Furthermore, after joining Mercy House as a live-in "core community" member, Paul was required to read the "welcome wagon" materials, which exposed new members to the activist works of Peter Maurin, Dorothy Day, and other social-justice writers.

Although the specifics of the socialization process varied, one feature was routine: volunteers were learning from each other. Although they could have developed opinions about homelessness and homeless service provision based on their interactions with those experiencing homelessness, interviewees indicated that other volunteers played a dominant role. My field observations confirmed that volunteers gave great weight to other volunteers' opinions and that conversations with the group at large served as opportunities to iron out common understand-

FIGURE 4. Street view showing a former Catholic church with Mercy House just behind the church, May 30, 2021. At the time of my fieldwork Mercy House served as a shelter for women, families, and transgender people. After my fieldwork concluded and after more than forty years as a Catholic Worker house, Mercy House closed and was gifted to another local nonprofit organization dedicated to "curing homelessness." © Matthew Jerome Schneider.

ings and service approaches. At times, this process took the form of jokes and stories, as was the case with Vincent and Gabriela. At other times, meaning was conveyed through casual conversation with, observation of, and dialogue with other volunteers, as was the case for Paul, Alena, and Veronica.

Finally, after volunteers had become socialized into the group, they expressed interest in maintaining their membership. When I asked Sixtus if something about homeless service provision had kept him working at Mercy House for more than twenty years, he cited the relationship to other volunteers. Although they might not have shared his precise views, they were like-minded people, and he thus felt at home at Mercy House:

> I'm always amazed when I think back on—that I've lived in St. Louis for the better part of thirty years. It just seems amazing. I didn't plan on being here that long. And I think the reason I stayed around was being involved in a community where—and probably most Catholic Workers will say some version of this— where you know you're not alone. When I lived [at Mercy House], when I came home, there were always people who if I started talking a little bit about how my day went—would have been thinking about that day or work on that day—

there's always somebody who would understand and get it. And the same thing me for them. If people came in, and we didn't all feel exactly the same way about everything, but we were very close in proximity about our heads and hearts and all that. So that really was something I needed. Probably still do. . . .

I think the work, and it happening alongside the community, is why I'm still around at Mercy House. I've met some really fine people and want to continue to meet really fine people here who come to share the work in some way. So I think all of that is why I'm still around. It's not *just* the work, it's the community. It's not *just* the community, it's the work, and it's all wrapped up.

The length of Sixtus's involvement was extreme, but the sentiment he conveyed was not. For the volunteers in this study, the work's meaning was amplified by the ability to do that work alongside other volunteers they knew, they could relate to, and they respected.

As Tom Knecht and Lisa M. Martinez (2009) have found, coming into contact with people experiencing homelessness did little to alter volunteers' beliefs about the government's response to homelessness although they became more likely to adopt structural views of homelessness after making contact. Focusing on meaning-making among volunteers, a process that starts even before joining the group, might help explain why exposure to homelessness does little to change ideas about the best way to address homelessness. Because volunteers were generally joining groups of like-minded people, their interaction with other volunteers generally strengthened and entrenched their existing opinions. For Fran, Sixtus, and Barbara, this process stretched for decades.

Producing Sin-Talk and Responses to "Sin"

The night of February 12 was not especially cold, but with the temperature hovering around thirty degrees Fahrenheit, it certainly was not comfortable either. In spite of the weather, Right Choice dedicated that Monday night to "doing good" by "sweeping the streets" for people experiencing homelessness in need of food, water, blankets, and/or clothes. In addition to the somewhat random and uneventful street sweep, we made a number of stops at known hangouts and camps for people experiencing homelessness—places where group members more or less knew who would be there. After several hours of service that included stops at a downtown shelter and a visit to "our homeless friends" at two separate camps east of the Mississippi River, most group members departed for home. At the suggestion of the group's white leader, John, however, I joined him and Gregory, another white volunteer, for a final stop on the North Side of the city. John wanted to visit

Stan, a tall, middle-aged white man who lived in a dilapidated warehouse. At the time, it was very important to John that Right Choice make regular contact with Stan because another member of the group, Raymond, whom I met only once, had identified Stan as someone who would be receptive to and benefit from a relationship with Right Choice.

When we arrived at the seemingly abandoned warehouse, John quickly walked up and rapped on a large metal door previously used for loading supplies onto delivery trucks. After a short silence, we heard someone working his way toward the door, and a moment later the large door loudly slid upward, revealing the gray-haired Stan. Toward the back of the dark, damp warehouse, we could see wood pallets being burned for warmth, surrounded by a handful of chairs, a mattress, and whatever junk had been abandoned with the building.

John explained who we were, told Stan that we were friends of Raymond, and asked if Stan wanted to talk. He did, motioning for us to enter the building. We hopped up and through the door, and Stan closed it behind us as we moved toward the fire. He told us to pull up a chair, and there was one for each of the four of us. As I sat quietly, thankful to be in front of the warm fire and observing that most of the roof was missing, John asked how Stan was getting along, whether he needed anything, how he had found the building, and whether he had any family. He answered all of John and Gregory's questions but generally kept the replies short and simple. Stan said that he was getting along fine; he was just waiting to find work, preferably in HVAC or doing assembly, as he had previously at Chrysler. He could use more coffee but otherwise did not need anything. A friend had scoped out the building in case they ever lost their space at the nearby shelter. Stan has a daughter in a southwest suburb but does not get to see her. Raymond had apparently been planning to pick Stan up for church the previous day, but they had missed each other, and John told Stan that Raymond was disappointed that it did not work out. John eventually announced that we would not take any more of Stan's time. Stan used his flashlight to guide us back to the door, and after we left, he slid the door shut behind us as we moved down the empty, dead-end street.

Standing out in the cold, the three of us had an excited conversation. John was quite encouraged by the interaction with Stan, who was surprisingly open: John had not expected Stan to invite us in or to share anything about his family life. John explained that he had emphasized Raymond's disappointment as a way to let Stan know that Raymond was interested and had made an effort to meet up. John could see why Raymond was drawn to Stan. Based on our short conversation, John claimed that he could see that Stan did not want to be on the streets and that he was "meek." People like Stan—or perhaps more accurately, John's interpretations of those people—were why he did this kind of volunteer work. John spent several minutes contrasting Stan, a supposedly motivated and deserving man who was down on his luck, to Enos and Willie, two other white men with whom group members regularly interacted and who they saw as too comfortable in their homelessness and as unwilling to work toward changing their lives. John repeatedly noted that a recent local documentary about homelessness in St. Louis featured Willie "on camera saying he *likes* living outside."

John again emphasized that he does this work because of the Stans of the world—the people he perceived as interested in working hard, staying clean, and finding permanent shelter: "I want to help those that want help. We didn't start this back in 2012 to see people stay where they're at." He did not want to give up on Enos and Willie, but they would not and could not be the center of his attention. Gregory did not advance the conversation but regularly echoed John's sentiments verbally and enthusiastically nodded his head as John talked, clearly demonstrating agreement.

Although volunteers did not exclude the possibility that homelessness might be linked to structural changes or social problems (e.g., layoffs as a result of changes in the economy or deindustrialization, as in Stan's case), they criticized people perceived as comfortably and immorally unhoused. Such "sin-talk" (Gowan 2010) was prevalent among volunteers in Right Choice Ministry. It was also common among members of Fellowship Outreach, although they more frequently blended their understanding of "sin" with "sick," and most Fellowship volunteers were considerably nicer when suggesting that homelessness was a lifestyle choice. John and Gregory reinforced the narrative of the deserving poor, situating many people experiencing homelessness as highly agentic but choosing to be poor rather than making the moral decision to pull themselves up by their bootstraps.

In addition, sin-talk among volunteer group members functioned as meaning-making. Both John and Gregory used a relatively brief and shallow interaction with Stan as evidence that Willie and Enos were bordering on a lost cause. That "evidence" was deployed selectively to confirm the volunteers' preexisting understandings of homelessness, and the truly meaningful interaction was that among volunteers rather than the interaction between volunteers and people experiencing homelessness. These conversations allowed members to cement their social understandings of homelessness through an ongoing process of socialization. Although actors are provided space in the conversation to offer competing discourse, structural constraints generally encouraged people to reinforce existing social patterns (e.g., popular homeless discourses) rather than to attempt to undermine or modify them (Goffman 1959).

Producing System-Talk and Responses to the System

Although Gowan (2010) and Lyon-Callo (2015) have noted that system-talk is
generally discouraged in the social service industry, it was rather common among
members of Citywide Outreach, Fam in the Streets, Mercy House, and Service
House. Members of these groups were often eager to discuss systemic racism
and structural inequalities (see chapter 3). Referencing a popular aphorism, Fran
framed homelessness as a consequence of structural barriers:

> People need to be able to get stuff without asking for it. . . . If you give someone
> a fish, you feed him for a day. You teach him how to fish, they'll eat for a lifetime.
> But if you give them access to the lake or river, they don't need your help at all!
> We won't even have to teach them how to fish. People have a right to access to
> those things. And so that's the gap. So I try to give access. That's why I always have
> to work for justice while doing charity.

Fran's analysis sharply contrasted with the viewpoint of more paternalistic volunteers, who felt that people experiencing homelessness needed someone to guide
them and help them make better choices. From Fran's perspective, people living in
extreme poverty needed access to resources such as health care, housing, and jobs
that should be freely available to everyone. With access to those resources, people experiencing homelessness would no longer need charity. Fran and others who
engaged in discourses of system-talk articulated homelessness as injustice resulting from systemic oppression and inequitable distribution of resources. However,
volunteers with this mindset also had no illusions regarding imminent change in
the social systems that discriminate against the poor and people of color. These
volunteers consequently embraced their roles as direct service providers while ex-
pressing frustration at their inability to focus on structural change because of the
never-ending stream of direct needs to address. Nevertheless, they did their best to
change the system.

On January 11, 2018, Fran penned an open letter to St. Louis mayor Lyda Krewson. Fran opened by reminding Krewson about two men who died of hypother-
mia during the winter of 2017–18—one found in a portable toilet and the other in
a dumpster. Fran wrote that although "the full responsibility for ending homelessness does not rest with the City," the government did bear responsibility for some
specific failures, among them the closing of the New Life Evangelistic Center:

> By taking this action, the City showed a preferential option to respond to those
> with money and power over those who have been left in poverty. One can debate
> much about the strengths and weaknesses of any shelter, including New Life, but

there is no denying that much of the reason for closing that shelter was to "protect" the business area around it from those who are unhoused. New Life stood unimpeded in its work for close to 40 years until the downtown became a more fashionable place to live and do business, making New Life's presence unwanted.

She also criticized the city for displacing people sleeping in tents and in parks and for reducing the budget of the Affordable Housing Trust fund by $500,000 per year. Fran also proposed a number of solutions, including the reopening of a walk-up emergency shelter, additional funding for the Affordable Housing Trust Fund, the establishment of a St. Louis Homeless Bill of Rights, and community dialogue. Fran viewed homelessness as a structural problem and sought institutional changes that would at least better meet the immediate needs of those experiencing homelessness and provide them with legal protections.

Fran's letter had important ramifications for Citywide Outreach and a handful of other collaborating groups (including Fam in the Streets and Mercy House). Fran's system-talk provided a roadmap for members of the group, communicating how they should understand and address homelessness. When members of Citywide and others gathered to discuss how to advocate for changes, they knew where to start discussion. When Mayor Krewson agreed to a May 2018 meeting with the group, activists held sessions to prepare. They decided to focus on demonstrating (1) that the police were criminalizing the unhoused (despite Mayor Krewson's insistence to the contrary) and (2) that it is more expensive to invest in public safety (e.g., police wages, emergency room bills, and court costs for tickets issued) than to invest in affordable public housing. Although the group never succeeded in obtaining commitments from Krewson, the shared experience in advocating for systemic change affirmed participants' belief that homelessness was a systemic problem. Their work was a social and political project (Omi and Winant 1994), simultaneously serving as an interpretation, representation, and explanation of homelessness.

Producing Sick-Talk and Responses to Sickness

Sick-talk such as that expressed by Gabriela regarding Miss Alberta occurred across all observed groups, most commonly in the form of conversations about alcoholism and drug addiction. Volunteers took a well-known fact—people experiencing homelessness have elevated risks for mental illness, alcoholism, and/or drug dependence (Fazel et al. 2008)—and used it to explain particular cases without much reflection or consideration of alternative possibilities. For example, on October 5, 2017, volunteers from Fellowship Outreach made their first stop of the night at a common meeting spot just outside the main downtown area of the city. Per usual, the group kicked things off by forming a circle to pray. Lou, an unhoused white man who frequently attended the weekly gatherings, offered to lead the prayer. In his prayers, he mentioned a friend who had recently suffered broken ribs during a mugging and as a result could not join the group gathering on that evening. Aside from this rather unfortunate news, the first stop was uneventful. Jude, an older white volunteer, wondered why the streetlights did not turn on until well past sunset. As young men on motorcycles roared up and down the relatively empty street, people commented on the noise and the danger of the tricks being performed. Alena showed me pictures of her dog. Once conversation began to peter out, volunteers made their way back to their cars. Jude and I rode in a car driven by Michael, another of Fellowship's most consistent members. Michael expressed surprise about the woman who had been mugged, adding, "They think it was drug related." Jude agreed without question and without advancing the conversation.

Just one day earlier, I had interviewed Jude one-on-one, and he had said that a "lot of" homelessness,

> from what I've seen, is drug related. Not necessarily drugs, but I consider alcohol a drug, too. I know quite a few of them are either full-blown alcoholics or addicts of one type or another. In fact, I'd say, without a doubt, most of them are. . . .
>
> I see the same group every week, so [my experience is limited]. But in that group, I guess there's . . . maybe fifty people, and I say most of them—alcohol, drugs, or maybe a past criminal history make getting a job hard. I see that a lot too.
>
> Now, that's my limited knowledge of their past. I really don't ask them a whole lot, but I know what I see. When [you ask where someone is], and they say, "Well, he's meeting his man right now to get his drugs," that's a pretty good indication.

Jude's qualifications about his "limited knowledge" highlight the speculative nature of these "causes" of homelessness. Rather than base his conclusion on conversations with people experiencing homelessness, he relied on a single example and then used it to explain a wide range of cases.

Jude and Michael affirmed their shared understanding of homelessness through intragroup discourse—in this case, sick-talk. Members of Fellowship Outreach as well as other groups frequently deployed alcoholism, drug addiction, and other forms of mental illness to "explain" cases ranging from joblessness to mugging. Perhaps unsurprisingly, this sort of discourse veered into sin-talk for members of Fellowship and Right Choice, with Jude one night openly pondering the idea that Gibby, a hardworking man with an "alcohol problem," would not put down the bottle to "better himself." But with this common understanding of the "causes" of homelessness in mind, Fellowship Outreach's leaders saw meeting people where they were as part of their mission. In Alena's explained view, most of the people living on the streets have some sort of mental issue—addiction, alcoholism, an intellectual disability, or some sort of "psychological hang-up." Consequently, Fellowship focused primarily on going out and talking to people who were waiting for a platform, for someone to listen to them tell their story, something that she believed "normal people don't need." This perception gave meaning to her group's mission: whether this sickness could be overcome (e.g., treatment for addiction) or was permanent (e.g., an intellectual disability), sick-talk helped volunteers frame and give purpose to their practices.

Making Meaning about Homelessness

Volunteering is often treated as an opportunity for volunteers to learn, to cross cultural barriers, and to alter their perspectives (Clary and Snyder 1999; Clayton and Ash 2004; Einfeld and Collins 2008). But given that the social and cultural gap between volunteers and service recipients often widens rather than shrinks over the course of service, shifts in volunteer perspective and practice cannot be assumed under all conditions (Godfrey et al. 2019; Raymond and Hall 2008; Simpson 2004; Sin 2009). In the case of homeless service provision, contact with people experiencing homelessness seems to affect understandings of homelessness as a social phenomenon, as Knecht and Martinez (2009) have shown.

Volunteer groups serve as a mechanism for reproducing understandings of homelessness and approaches to homeless service provision. As volunteers become socialized into groups, the process either affirms existing understandings of homelessness or helps people learn to see homelessness in a way that meshes with the group's common discourse and with the "wisdom" of mentors and senior group leaders. Little research has directly explored practices of volunteering (J. Wilson 2012), but social interaction among volunteers in many ways resembles most other forms of social interaction. Volunteering must first and foremost be understood as a practice of meaning-making (Blumer 1969; G. H. Mead 1962). In particular, this process focuses on learning who and how to serve, on developing an understanding of homelessness. Volunteers are prompted by their peers to entrench or revise understandings of what homelessness means. What "causes" homelessness? How can homelessness be best addressed? Although the finding that volunteering is a form of meaning-making may be unsurprising, it lays the groundwork for the finding that socialization allows volunteers not only to build common understandings of homelessness but also to frame, justify, and inform their continued volunteer work. In a more abstract sense, volunteer missions and discourses highlight the structural limitations of their positions.

Sin-talk, system-talk, and sick-talk are social constructions in their own right that communicate meaning to social subjects (e.g., volunteers attempting to navigate homeless and urban spaces) (Saussure 2011). While volunteers could conceivably generate their own understandings about homelessness, their actions and opinions are ultimately modeled after or alongside those of other group members. To be sure, volunteers possess understandings of the meaning of homelessness when joining groups and would be unlikely to stay with a group that espoused an unpalatable message. However, volunteers also speak of their respect for mentors and other volunteers, especially with regard to framing the group's work.

Volunteers navigate a structural context. While scholars of social inequalities note the structural barriers that people experiencing homelessness are likely to encounter as they seek employment, housing, and social services, the cultural and policy context likewise influences volunteer action. Volunteers have agency and could leverage their experiences to challenge existing cultural understandings of poverty and homelessness. However, they generally choose from the menu of options placed before them, selecting explanations of poverty and service practices endorsed by people with whom the volunteers identify. In so doing, they collectively help to reproduce and legitimate the existing structural context.

CHAPTER 2

"I Think It Is a Little Bit of an Issue of Being Able to Connect"

Excerpt of an Interview with Lawrence White,
Middle-Class Volunteer with Right Choice
Ministry and Outreach
May 31, 2018

Matt (Interviewer): Have you noticed when you're out doing service work, do you feel like race ever informs the way people interact?

Lawrence: I think with our group it doesn't. Yeah. I don't think it affects our group at all.

Matt: Why is that? Why do you think your group is able to skate around this issue?

Lawrence: I think we're really down-to-earth people. It's a good question. I think John especially is able to look at everybody. . . . I think John's a great person. I don't think he cares about who you are or whatever. He's willing to help out anybody, and I think that definitely plays into it.

Matt: What about you?

Lawrence: For me personally, I think that there is—I mean, definitely in my mind—there is a little bit of race issue. Not enough that I want it to be there, but I think just because of life that it is a little bit of it is there for me. But I keep coming out, and it's pretty much nonexistent now.

Matt: So what is the issue in your mind? Is it an issue with people of color or is it something else?

Lawrence: I think it is a little bit of an issue of being able to connect, because I think that maybe there might be some issue in their mind on the other end. I think that that is always something that I think about.

Matt: So you think you might be perceived differently than a Black volunteer, for example?

Lawrence: Yes. I think that plays into it.

Matt: Do you ever feel like you are treated differently?

Lawrence: Honestly, from all the people that I've met, no. I don't think that we are.

Matt: Let me rephrase my question. Can you imagine if the color of your skin was different, if you were Black, do you think that [your] relationship with [Black men experiencing homelessness] would look different?

Lawrence: I think the relationship would look different, yeah. I think there might be a little more closeness, a more level playing field if I was [Black]. I think that whole group [on the North Side], we might be perceived—I know that we would be perceived a little bit different.

Matt: What do you mean by a level playing field?

Lawrence: I think there is still that if we were Black, I think that it would be more acceptance, I guess. Just more accepted.

Matt: But there's still some sort of hesitation that you perceive?

Lawrence: I definitely think there is a little bit, yeah.

Matt: What about homelessness as a social issue? Is race at all intertwined with causes of homelessness?

Lawrence: I don't think so, because we see people of every race, culture, all walks of life. I think it affects everybody.

Matt: What are the common causes of homelessness do you think?

Lawrence: In my opinion, I think it could be just—it's their way of life. It's the only way of life they've known. That's the only life that they want. . . . A lot of people say they don't understand how people get to where they are, and I don't know everybody's situation out there, but some people choose it, and some people it just kind of happens. I know a lot of times for myself, if I didn't have my family to help me, I could easily be in the same spot.

(The Limits of) Charity

"Enabling," Color Blindness, and the Reproduction of Stigma

Few volunteers would claim that race is irrelevant or that racism is dead in St. Louis. Still, color-blind ideologies framed the way volunteers from Fellowship Outreach and Right Choice Ministry and Outreach perceived and interacted with the world. A number of volunteers declared that being color-blind was a personal goal. Color-blind ideology, generally speaking, removes "from personal thought and public discussion any taint or suggestion of white supremacy or white guilt while legitimating the existing social, political and economic arrangements which privilege whites" (Gallagher 2003, 22), and volunteers deployed the frames of color-blind racism selectively to mute consideration of their role in the reproduction of racial inequality.

This chapter delves into the beliefs, attitudes, and practices of service groups characterized by their color-blind ideologies. Both of this study's groups in this category were Protestant Christian organizations (as the literature suggests [Edgell and Tranby 2007; Emerson and Smith 2000]), and their service practices were built around acts of charity (i.e., they focused on "handouts" and relief through connection and/or prayer). In this context, volunteers viewed homelessness as an individual failing, a consequence of laziness, or an issue of personal choice. By emphasizing the morality of work (Gowan 2010) and individual choice (Parsell and Parsell 2012; Snow and Anderson 1993), volunteers reproduced classed ideas about deservingness as a way of justifying service practices (Froyum 2018). That said, questions about deservingness did not occur in a vacuum. Ideas about race were intertwined with ideas about class. These groups exhibited patterns of color-blind racism, and color-blind ideologies shape patterns of service interaction: predominantly white groups of people experiencing homelessness were observed to benefit from friendlier relationships, frequent volunteer visits, and perhaps more "handouts."

Charity and the Deserving Poor

Although many Americans still participate in collective forms of civic engagement such as social protest and union membership, individual-level volunteering is among the most popular forms of civic engagement, perhaps second only to voting. According to the U.S. Department of Labor's Bureau of Labor Statistics (2016), about 62.6 million people in the United States (about 24.9 percent of the total population) volunteered for an organization between September 2014 and September 2015, with each person providing a median of fifty-two hours of labor. The Charities Aid Foundation (2017) provides a more liberal estimate, reporting that 41 percent of people in the United States volunteered for an organization in 2016. The United States ranks seventh in the world among percentages of people volunteering, and according to the foundation's World Giving Index—a score based on rates of volunteering, donation, and helping strangers—the United States ranked as the world's fifth-most-generous country in 2016.

Prior to the 1970s, civic engagement would have been best defined as public group action and discourse intended to address what might otherwise be seen as individual-level problems. In more recent decades, Michael X. Delli Carpini (2000, 346) and other scholars have observed that "civic engagement has become defined as the one-on-one experience of working in a soup kitchen, cleaning trash from a local river, or tutoring a child once a week." While public interest in and mobilization around systemic issues continues, especially as the climate movement and Black Lives Matter push on, much of this work has been professionalized. In consequence, opportunities for people to involve themselves with system-facing, grassroots organizations are not as available as they were in the mid-twentieth century (Fisher 2006; Skocpol 1999). But even if individual-oriented forms of civic engagement occupy a more prominent place in American society than they did in the past, these forms of helping are not new. They build on a strong Christian tradition of charity. Social work scholar Bruce D. Friedman (2002, 4) argues that "both the Judeo and Christian traditions use the term charity to describe patterns of welfare, but charity is defined differently by each. These differences have led to a dichotomy in the forms assumed by helping traditions in the United States." In the Jewish tradition, *tzedakah*, the Hebrew word for "charity," also means "justice" or "righteousness." Charity in the Jewish tradition is understood as a set of goods and services to which all community members are entitled. In the Christian tradition, however, charity, derived from the Latin word *caritas*, translates as "love." While this tradition is not at odds with the need to develop better systems of resource distribution, it emphasizes "a very individualized approach to addressing the needs of the poor" (9). Indeed, all the volunteer groups with which I worked engaged in practices designed to meet the direct needs of St. Louis's unhoused population, and doing so was the primary emphasis of Right Choice and Fellowship.

However, not all "homeless friends" received the same level of charity from these groups. A single group of grassroots volunteers cannot meet the direct needs of hundreds of people experiencing homelessness on any given night, meaning that the group must have a way to determine who to help and how to do so. Alongside its long history of charity and civic engagement, the United States has a lengthy tradition of determining which people experiencing poverty are deemed deserving.

The U.S. welfare system, for example, was reformed under the Bill Clinton administration based on long-standing cultural ideas about deservingness and vulnerability (Edin and Shaefer 2015; Moffitt 2015). The 1996 welfare reform package, Temporary Assistance for Needy Families, formalized the dominant cultural narrative that work is a moral obligation for all those considered able. Instead of having government support sustain generations of consistently poor Americans, strict limits would be placed on eligibility. To give welfare recipients a "hand up, not a handout" (Somers and Block 2005), they were required to actively apply for jobs (Edin and Shaefer 2015; Moffitt 2015). Over the ensuing three decades, aid has increasingly been funneled to those deemed deserving, especially the elderly and those with disabilities, while less aid is routed to single-parent households and those with the lowest incomes in favor of support for two-parent households and households with higher incomes (Moffitt 2015). Even as policies force people experiencing poverty into low-wage and precarious work, American myths about the (un)deserving poor remain strong. Furthermore, federal guidelines encourage local homeless service organizations to prioritize vulnerable and deserving "target populations": families with children, people who are chronically homeless, and veterans (Osborne 2019). People experiencing homelessness who do not fit into these categories are often assumed to be "choosing homelessness," without consideration for the structural context in which those choices are made. Indeed, this assumption has informed social policy (Parsell and Parsell 2012). As Melissa Osborne (2019, 404) puts it, "This system has produced a climate where merely being homeless is no longer enough to be considered sufficiently vulnerable for receiving housing."

This situation is not strictly a matter of top-down policy implementation. Individual volunteers and employees in social services work with these cultural understandings of deservingness and poverty in mind. Volunteering is motivated and sustained by volunteers' ability to see recipients as deserving of services, and volunteers regularly gauge the neediness, blamelessness, and impressionability of the individuals they serve (Froyum 2018). Indeed, a fair amount of research suggests that these narratives about deservingness often intertwine with the expressed missions of faith-based Christian service organizations. Jason Hackworth (2012), for example, draws largely on observations of George W. Bush–era politics and the nonprofit response to Hurricane Katrina to argue that (evangelical) faith-based organizations have gained support from the Right because of their frequent focus on personal responsibility. Even if faith-based charity has not wholly replaced the American welfare system, it is a popular goal in neoliberal America because it emphasizes that no one is entitled to aid. Similarly, Daniel Bolger's (2022) study of Christian social service agencies finds that organizations construct stories about who deserves services and that these narratives inform resource distribution. The organizations developed group understandings about what it means to be in need, with groups trying to filter out service recipients who would "take advantage of the system" or who were "less-than-needy" (81). Jason Adam Wasserman and Jeffrey M. Clair (2010) similarly observe that Christian service groups and religious institutions, which lead a majority of homeless service projects in the United States, deploy Calvinistic notions of work and morality in a way that stigmatizes the unhoused. In this way, volunteering and other forms of service provision serve as an arena in which providers simultaneously benefit from feelings of generosity and engage in boundary work that reinforces cultural stereotypes and the social distance between themselves and people experiencing homelessness (Rogers 2017).

These boundaries are not (re)produced in a vacuum. Historical, cultural, and structural context matter, and class(ism) and race(ism) are inseparable in these contexts (Crenshaw 1991; Feagin 2013; Hall et al. 1978; Omi and Winant 1994). The "culture of poverty" arguments that served as a driving philosophy of the 1996 welfare reform, for example, work in service to white supremacy by framing higher rates of intergenerational poverty, single-parent households, and incarceration as evidence of Black cultural failings rather than as structural outcomes (e.g., D'Souza 1995; L. E. Harrison 1992; L. Mead 1992; Moynihan 1965). In addition, Americans and especially white Americans are more likely to turn to narratives about individual achievement and hard work in the interest of white supremacy (DeSante 2013; Federico and Sidanius 2002; Kinder and Sanders 1996; Samson

2013; Thornhill 2019; T. C. Wilson 2006), and social service organizations are less likely to be located in poor and/or minority neighborhoods, even when the mission of those organizations is to serve poor and/or minority communities (Allard 2009; K. F. Anderson 2017; Bolger 2021). In what ways, then, do ideas about race intertwine with ideas about deservingness of people experiencing poverty? How do racial ideologies affect service provision? Volunteer tourists' understandings of race help create and maintain networks of relatively exclusive white spaces in nonwhite countries even as volunteers profess an interest in cultural immersion (Schneider 2018), and service projects often reproduce narratives of white saviorhood without undermining the systems that produce and maintain racialized inequality (Cann and McCloskey 2017; Droogendyk et al. 2016; Endres and Gould 2009; Hanchey 2018). Color-blind ideology intertwines with and complements popular volunteer narratives about deservingness and individualistic approaches to the problem of homelessness.

Color Blindness and Protestantism

Following the civil rights movement, racial attitudes began to shift dramatically, and by the 1980s, Americans were rarely willing to express explicitly racist attitudes on surveys regarding issues such as school and residential segregation, intermarriage, and employment discrimination (Schuman, Steeh, and Bobo 1985). Instead, racism took a turn toward subtlety, with the "color-blind perspective" insinuating "that class and culture, and not institutional racism, are responsible for social inequality" (Gallagher 2003, 26). Color blindness does not mean that race is perceived as inconsequential. Color-blind whites do take notice of race, and race does communicate meaningful symbols to color-blind actors (Bonilla-Silva 2010; Krysan 2015; Lewis 2001, 2003). People who engage with the world based on color-blind ideologies are less likely to act against racial prejudice (Yi, Todd, and Mekawi 2019), with this inaction justified by a worldview that recognizes patterns of racial inequality but explains away the importance of racism as social force that continues to produce such outcomes.

Eduardo Bonilla-Silva (2010) argues that color-blind racism operates through four ideological frames that can be employed singularly or in combination: abstract liberalism, naturalization, cultural racism, and minimization of racism. The abstract liberalism frame can be understood as an attempt to justify racism by misrepresenting the ideals of liberalism. Through this frame, color-blind Americans espouse notions of equal opportunity, choice, and freedom to oppose progressive social policies such as affirmative action and to dismiss racial inequalities such as segregated neighborhoods. "By framing race-related issues in the language of liberalism, whites can appear 'reasonable' and even 'moral,' while opposing almost all practical approaches to deal with de facto racial inequality" (28). The naturalization frame "allows whites to explain away racial phenomena by suggesting they are natural occurrences" (28). Segregation and social inequality are dismissed as "just the way things are" (Bonilla-Silva, Goar, and Embrick 2006, 240), unavoidable, or simply the result of wanting to be near people like themselves (Bonilla-Silva 2010; Burke 2012). The cultural racism frame argues that existing racial inequalities can be attributed to cultural inferiority. When whites cannot explain away existing inequalities, they often turn to common stereotypes and tropes about minority cultures, making claims like "'Mexicans do not put much emphasis on education' or 'blacks have too many babies' to explain the standing of minorities in society" (Bonilla-Silva 2010, 28). The minimization-of-racism frame is based on the suggestion that "discrimination is no longer a central factor affecting minorities' life chances" (29), facilitating the argument that success can be attained by working hard and that "playing the race card" is an "excuse" for personal or minority-cultural failures.

While the literature indicates that whites interacting in predominantly non-white spaces tend to become more aware of their whiteness/difference (Gallagher 1995, 1997; Schneider 2018), their ideological outlooks do not necessarily change across settings. For example, sociologist Meghan Burke (2012, 25) finds that even among liberal whites living in "stably diverse" communities, "residents are both color-blind and pro-diversity." In other words, while white residents expressed an interest in maintaining their communities' racial diversity, they often undermined this sentiment through expressions of color-blind racism. Whites in these diverse communities commonly expressed cultural racism (e.g., "Black families do not care about the well-being of their children"), naturalization (e.g., "Minority groups choose to segregate themselves"), and minimization of racism (e.g., "Race used to be an issue, but any persistent inequalities are class-based, not racial"). Despite their color-consciousness, these whites selectively and regularly invoked three of Bonilla-Silva's (2010) frames of color blindness.

The pervasiveness of color-blind ideologies has come with a rule book of sorts that regulates speech, policy, and interactions. The near ubiquity of color-blind ideologies has set rather strict boundaries on discourse that sometimes impair effective communication (Norton et al. 2006) or encourage whites to skirt important racialized social problems (Burke 2012). Burke finds that expectations of color-blind discourse prevented her pro-diversity participants from engaging with the subject of race even in mundane ways. Instead, whites speak in (often racist) coded talk as a way of adhering to a "color-blind rubric" for discourse while still discussing race (2012, 91; Myers 2005). Furthermore, incoherent talk "underscores the desire to say something outside of the bounds of legitimate discourse, something real and important to the actors in concrete environments" (Burke 2012, 92).

Navigating a world regulated by the rules of color blindness can affect the behaviors and interactions of people of color as well. Daniel Burdsey (2011), for example, finds that British Asian cricket players endure various forms of racism from teammates but regularly dismiss the prejudice as "banter" to ease navigation through their social world. To do otherwise would breach the boundaries of appropriate color-blind discourse. As one player put it, British Asian players "don't want to make an issue of it just in case it blows out of proportion, so a lot of it is then just quashed and, you know, pushed aside" (271). Furthermore, color-blind social environments can take a toll on the psychological well-being of people of color (Plaut, Thomas, and Goren 2009) and promote or justify racial and ethnic discrimination (Apfelbaum, Sommers, and Norton 2008; Knowles et al. 2009; Saguy, Dovidio, and Pratto 2008).

Scholars of race and religion have shown that understandings of race and poverty are tied to religious ideology, with white evangelicals more likely to interpret the world through a color-blind lens emphasizing meritocratic ideals. Conversely, Catholics are more likely to be sympathetic to structural limitations and to support state welfare policies (Edgell and Tranby 2007; Emerson and Smith 2000; Tranby and Hartmann 2008; VanHeuvelen 2014). Given that religious organizations operate the majority of homeless service projects (Wasserman and Clair 2010), it is important to be attentive to the way religious ideologies work in conjunction with racial ideologies, racial status, and class status in volunteer settings. Penny Edgell and Eric Tranby (2007) complicate the relationship between religious subculture and racial attitudes/beliefs with their finding that gender, education, and race work in conjunction with religious involvement to shape beliefs about racial inequality. Hispanic Catholics and African Americans with orthodox religious beliefs are more likely than other groups to attribute racial inequality to structural causes. Similarly, Tranby and Douglas Hartmann (2008) argue that the individualism espoused by evangelical Christians "blinds white evangelicals to structural inequalities involving race" (Tranby and Hartmann 2008, 342; see also Emerson and Smith 2000). Tranby and Hartmann extend this line of thinking by arguing that this individualism "also assigns blame to those who are disadvantaged by race and normalizes and naturalizes cultural practices, beliefs, and norms that privilege white Americans over others" (342). Because volunteering often takes place through religious institutions (Hackworth 2012; Wasserman and Clair 2010), is more common among whites (Foster-Bey 2008; Rotolo, Wilson, and Hughes 2010), and is crucial to meeting the needs of the poor, these connections merit further exploration.

Charity: Volunteer Understandings of Homelessness and the Value of Fellowship

Views on homelessness and opinions about appropriate responses to homelessness are not monolithic in the United States. On the one hand, the public expresses substantial support for policies that exclude people experiencing homelessness from public space (Clifford and Piston 2017). On the other hand, recent surveys have shown that public attitudes toward those experiencing homelessness have become more compassionate and politically liberal in recent years. In particular, Americans increasingly favor governmental support for people experiencing homelessness (Clifford and Piston 2017; Tsai et al. 2017, 2019). These attitudes are not mutually exclusive. Beliefs about poverty and how governments should respond do not fall neatly into "conservative" and "liberal" platforms (Robinson 2009), and many of those who support exclusionary policies that target the unhoused are not significantly less likely to support homeless aid policies (Clifford and Piston 2017). Tom Knecht and Lisa M. Martinez (2009) have found that the experiences of volunteers who came into contact with people experiencing homelessness did little to change opinions about how the government should respond to the problem of homelessness even as those interactions encouraged structuralist explanations of homelessness.

The volunteer groups highlighted in this chapter embody this tension. Although Fellowship and Right Choice members did not necessarily rule out the potential negative impacts of racism, discrimination, and other structural mechanisms of inequality, their approach to service prioritized charity and one-on-one or small-group interaction. This tension was regularly on the minds of some volunteers, including Peter, a white man and one of Fellowship Outreach's two leaders. Peter saw Fellowship Outreach's "greater mission" as

> basically to become a conduit between homeless people and sponsors—be it individuals, churches, or corporations—who are willing to sponsor homeless people out of homelessness. That's the ultimate goal. What we're doing right now—basically, we're putting a Band-Aid on an issue. Now and then, we're able to help people get into housing or get on a bus and get out of town back to their family, stuff like that, and that's beautiful. And that's rich, rewarding work. But for the

most part, 90 percent of what we're doing [providing food and supplies], we're putting a Band-Aid [on the problem]. At the same time, like I say, we're developing a relationship—finding out what pieces are missing for folks to get off of the streets, and occasionally we're able to be that. But ultimately the goal of Fellowship Outreach would be to be that conduit between the homeless people and the sponsors, manage that relationship. In most metro areas—and this is what inspired me, inspired that vision: a friend of mine who's very involved in homeless services told me that most metro areas, there's more churches than there are homeless people and that if each church would take on one homeless person, we could end homelessness for the most part in this country in most of the cities. So with that in mind, I thought, "We're out here. We're on the streets. I know so many homeless folks. I could be that person to hook the homeless person up with the person who has the ability to sponsor them out of homelessness."

In Peter's vision, sponsors would provide funds to house people.

We can talk about mental illness, drug abuse, alcoholism—these are things that you see with homeless people—with a lot of them. But basically, the problem is [that] with homelessness, they don't have a home. If they all had a home, they wouldn't be homeless, right? Some of the folks I met, you could probably put them in a house and two months later, they'd be back on the streets, because they don't possess the IQ or they have mental issues that won't allow them to do the things that need to be done to maintain being housed. So they would need a different kind of help. But like I say, that's the ultimate goal, is to help individuals, churches, and corporations take on the problem of homelessness.

Peter integrates multiple narratives into his analysis of homelessness and his group's responses to it. Despite his recognition that no sufficient system exists to respond to the most basic problem of homelessness, he centers narratives about sick talk and the need for relationship building. Even if Fellowship created a new system for the St. Louis area, the group's missions both present and future would rely on making connections and fostering relationships with individuals experiencing homelessness.

Right Choice similarly emphasized the need for intimate and direct connections between individuals volunteering and those experiencing homelessness. On my first night observing the group, January 30, 2018, John, a white man and group leader, spoke with me at length about his views on homelessness. As we drove around the city to visit his "homeless friends," he confidently explained how many people were homeless because they had made poor choices. As I reflected in my field notes,

FIGURE 5. A volunteer provides a hot meal to a man staying at the city shelter as other volunteers socialize down the street, June 3, 2021. © Matthew Jerome Schneider.

Although John acknowledged that some people are on the streets because of their "mental capacity," his opinion seems to be that homelessness is about the choices people make. He spoke of people who refused to change, of people who waste their disability checks on alcohol and drugs. In turn, his purpose as an outreacher is first to make connections, second to get to know them, and third to help guide them to become "productive members of society" and "make better choices."

He expressed some frustration that he and others put a lot of time into making these connections and getting to know them but often are let down. He spoke of two men he got to know really well over Bible study at the [fast food restaurant] near [downtown] as an example of what often happens. According to John, even after spending time with them once a week, helping guide them, trying to help them change their life course, "one's behind bars and the other moved across the country."

Like Peter, John emphasized the importance of relationship-building at the same time that he expressed frustration with the group's inability to "change situations." With the exception of people with mental illness, he understood homelessness as resulting when people either explicitly chose to forgo shelter or, more commonly, made poor life decisions. His explanations located the problem of homelessness within the individual, meaning that the appropriate response was to work one-on-one with people experiencing homelessness, serving as a sort of moral guide along the path to becoming "productive members of society." John regularly encouraged Right Choice volunteers to "pick someone to form a relationship with," as he put it. Volunteers were expected to be proactive in cultivating one-on-one relationships and then to provide advice or mentoring with the goal of helping people out of homelessness. In his view, people experiencing homelessness "need someone to care about them, someone to journey with them, someone to help them make different choices to redirect their path, and bringing them to church has been fantastic for that."

Because Peter and John were group leaders, their perspectives carried a lot of weight. Volunteers often pointed to these two men as role models, and they set the tone for their groups by drawing on a rich Christian tradition of conceptualizing charity not just as direct giving but also as an act in which "one individual helps another as an expression of love" (Friedman 2002, 6). Because Peter and John saw homelessness as a matter of sickness or sin, of illness or choice, they sought to make intimate connections. The solution to homelessness was to physically, mentally, and emotionally shepherd each person down the correct path. Through their service practices, they participated in a larger project that redefined civic engagement and volunteering as a one-on-one experience rather than as work that would ultimately reorganize community institutions or undermine systems of oppression (Delli Carpini 2000, 346).

"Enabling" Homelessness

Many volunteers saw the individual-level approach taken by Right Choice and Fellowship as having limitations and risks. But where I and perhaps Peter might ask how their face-to-face service is situated within a larger framework designed to create opportunities for stable housing, gainful employment, and access to affordable health care, volunteers were more often concerned about "enabling" people to be homeless. As Jude, a white volunteer, explained, homeless outreach is

> something to do that's good. I don't do too much that's good. But now that I'm retired, I don't have a whole lot of activities, so I definitely do have enough time to do a little bit of good if I can....
>
> Like Peter says ... just trying to spread some communication, give them somebody to talk to, a hug—that seems to go a long way. I'm not sure we do *a whole* lot of good, but I think we do a little. I'm not sure we do a whole lot of good, to tell you the truth. In fact, there may be some cases where we're enabling them to

stay in that situation where they—if they can get free food four nights a week, they may not have to work for it. That's a factor, too, that I have to consider. But I guess I do it to meet them as much as them to meet me. Maybe it does me as much good as it does them. . . .

Hopefully what we're doing isn't a substitute for them to take any initiative and maybe getting a job that they can support themselves with. Like that line about giving a guy a fish, you feed him once; you teach him how to fish, you feed him forever.

Echoing the concerns of conservative politicians such as Ronald Reagan and Bill Clinton who blamed the welfare system for continued poverty (Edin and Shaefer 2015), volunteers often verbalized the fear that their work might encourage dependence. Alongside a desire to help, volunteers expressed a skepticism that reflected larger narratives about poverty. Who was deserving of their aid, and who would be enabled by it?

Volunteers regularly reflected about whether they were properly serving those who were the most vulnerable and/or deserving (Bolger 2022; Froyum 2018). Ideas about the morality of work and about personal determination (or the lack thereof) were popular ways of explaining who was deserving of aid and volunteers' time. Several outreach groups, including Right Choice and Fellowship, frequently visited Willie and Enos, two charismatic white men who had been persistently homeless for years. Their well-known record of homelessness meant that they received frequent criticism.[1] Bernard, an especially blunt white volunteer with Fellowship, explained,

I like going over to the camp with the campfire. Those guys are good guys for the most part. Really don't care for Willie all that much—got the beard, talks a lot. But I like Enos, and Kyle's a good guy. I like that he keeps a clean camp and all that. I still think, like all these folks, most of them are full of shit, you know. . . .

[Enos] keeps a good camp, a clean camp, keeps the addicts out. [He says], "From time to time, I'll have a beer or whatever," but [that's] bullshit, man—every time I come over here you smell like a damn brewery. You reek of booze. So don't try to shoot the piss, make it sound like you're not at least a former alcoholic. You know? Why are you homeless then? Because you're a smart guy. You say you do mechanic work. When you start dealing with these folks, you really see how far it really is to fall from being poor to homeless. It takes *a lot*, in my opinion. A lot. You really have to fuck up to be homeless in this society, in America. You really have to do a number on yourself to get there.

Who do we not see? You don't see the middle-class guy working a job, loses his job, and now he's out on the streets. You don't see that, right? Because that guy didn't smoke meth, wasn't using heroin, wasn't an alcoholic, was not involved in crime, was not lazy. He's a hardworking American and figures it out. Even if he has to sell his house and all his shit and go mow lawns, he figures it out, and makes sure he's not homeless and provides for his family. That's what the hardworking American does. These folks don't want to do that.

Bernard enjoyed his interactions with Enos but ultimately insisted that persistent homelessness could only be explained by personal failings. People of any race who were poor must be "involved in crime," "lazy," or supporting a drug habit: "You really have to fuck up to be homeless in this society." In contrast, "the hardworking American . . . figures it out."

Willie and Enos served as concrete examples volunteers could use to support their claims about homelessness being a choice or a lifestyle. In this way, Willie, Enos, and other white people experiencing homelessness had "marked" racial identities despite being white (Newitz and Wray 1996). Although these men benefited from friendly and relatively generous relationships with predominantly white volunteer groups, their class status conceivably "conferred a sense of failure for having not lived up to the affluent, suburban, privileged connotations of whiteness" (McDermott 2006, 2).

These individuals also provided volunteers with a mechanism for distancing themselves from discussions of the role white supremacy plays in producing racialized poverty. Despite the volunteers' frequent criticisms of Willie and Enos, members of both groups liked and connected with the men, viewed them as "good guys," and regularly visited them. Not everyone received such benefit of the doubt.

Color-Blind Underpinnings

There are myriad pathways for any given individual to become homeless. Social scientists, however, generally try to understand the ways in which homelessness is produced at a structural level—through the housing market, the care industry, and so on (Lyon-Callo 2015; Main 1998; Mitchell 2020; Willse 2015). For both Fellowship and Right Choice, these ideological underpinnings relied on lay observations of race, class, and urban space, all of them working in conjunction. Volunteers trying to interpret their encounters with people experiencing homelessness relied on (often stereotypical) notions of race and of Blackness in particular.

Ana, a white volunteer, connected individually oriented service to the classic expression of color blindness:

That's our whole point of being there, is to just love our neighbors. . . . If someone's extending their hand to help—I think if someone had an issue with skin
color, they just have no business volunteering. Do you know what I'm saying? I
take that back. People have business volunteering. I want everyone to volunteer.
That is just great. I just feel like [skin color] shouldn't be an issue. It's not an issue
for me, and I don't think it's an issue for any of the people that I've ever served
with. I could be wrong. I don't want to speak for them, but from what I can see,
it doesn't matter. . . . It's such a hard question to ask. It really is. It's a hard-to-ask
question, especially here in St. Louis. It doesn't bother me any. Like, me personally, you could be purple.

Although Ana acknowledged the existence of open questions about race and racism, she did not feel that they were "an issue" for anyone in Right Choice. To her,
a person's race did not matter, and she wanted only to "love our neighbors." Color
blindness, at least in a general sense of the word, was ideal. This understanding of

TABLE 1
Excerpt of interview with Ana, a lower middle-class white
volunteer, coded with color-blind racism themes.

I just, I know how I feel about it doesn't matter. *I don't care what color a person's skin is.* I don't care. But, it's also—*I also have thoughts on it, and they're not necessarily right.*	*rules of color-blind discourse*
Not that they're wrong. I just—they're my own thoughts, and there are some things that I'm OK with. I don't need to talk them out loud. . . . Do you know what I'm saying? I think I	*"incoherence"*
just went in a circle and didn't make any sense at all. I just, *I think a lot of it is the way they're raised.* A lot of [stumbles], a person is raised, not Blacks in general, just a person is raised, you know, it could have an effect, too, if you grew up in a poverty-stricken home. A lot of people pick up what they're taught. Do you know what I'm saying? A lot of people pick up those habits. . . . Habits like—just the	*cultural racism*
way that they are. *So if you see someone who is disrespectful, and you're around someone that's disrespectful all the time, you're probably going to be disrespectful yourself.* You think	*cultural racism, minimization of racism*
that's right, right? Yeah. And so that person could be disrespectful at a job and lose his job. Do you know what I'm saying? Just a lot of it is the way someone was raised. A lot of it could be circumstantial. I really don't know why [Blacks account for such a high percentage of homeless individuals], and I don't want to assume that I know why, that a lot of them, or some of them are—70 percent Black. I don't know why. *Each person is different. Each person has gone through their own problems and their own difficulties and struggles and just can't really touch base.*	*individualization of poverty*

racism locates the problem within the individual and limits racism to naked prejudice based on skin color. But color-blind whites do in fact take notice of race, and
race does communicate meaningful symbols to color-blind actors (e.g., Bonilla-
Silva 2010; Krysan 2015; Lewis 2001, 2003).

Fellowship and Right Choice volunteers frequently deployed the color-blind
tool kit. Ana's subsequent comments clearly demonstrated that race influenced
her understanding of her service and those she served, particularly when I asked
her to explain why African Americans might be overrepresented in St. Louis's annual point-in-time count. As table 1 shows, after invoking the rules of color-blind
discourse by noting that she does not "care what color a person's skin is," Ana immediately doubled back to observe that race can affect life opportunities, even if
she lacked the tools to clearly articulate the problem or to interpret the structural
nature of racialized poverty. She deployed the cultural racism frame, explaining
racialized poverty as a cultural characteristic cultivated through the child-rear-
ing practices of Black families in poverty. She pointed to assumed cultural habits/
flaws that are likely to result in unemployment. She then muddied the waters by
suggesting that each person is different, thereby failing to acknowledge if not undermining explanations relating to segregation, discrimination, and/or disinvest-
ment in poor and minority communities. Although she indicated that she asso-
ciates poverty with Blackness (Kirschenman and Neckerman 1991; Loury 2002),
she did not see race or racism as explaining racial inequality. For Ana, the problem
of poverty ultimately lies at the feet of each individual experiencing it.

Connection with Whom?

Despite volunteers' common claim that race did not matter and did not affect relationships or service behavior, I regularly noticed that race predicted the nature
of the services provided. Most obviously, color-blind groups spent little time on
St. Louis's predominantly Black North Side, but race influenced service provision in more subtle ways as well. Fellowship Outreach, for example, was among
the most routine-oriented groups with which I worked. We visited more or less
the same stops on the same day each week. The locations included common gathering or sleeping places such as abandoned buildings or church pavilions as well
as places that had one or a handful of tents and a firepit. At each stop, we would
share food, drinks, and supplies with those who needed it, and in line with Fellowship's mission we would make conversation in the name of "fellowship." I initially
found the friendliness woven into these interactions heartwarming.

Yet over the following weeks and months, I noticed that the degree of cama-
raderie varied from stop to stop, as did the racial makeup of the groups we vis-

ited. The first night's interactions almost exclusively involved white volunteers and white people experiencing homelessness. On subsequent nights, we often concluded our outreach at a church on the near South Side. A group of as many as twenty men, most of them Black, would have set up for the night, some lying on the church steps, others with blankets spread across picnic tables beneath a pavilion to the left of the church, and a few others tucked against the church's red brick exterior walls. By the time we parked and exited our cars, a few people would be moving to greet us and to collect whatever we had to offer. Interactions were never tense or unpleasant, but the conversations rarely lasted very long. Most of the men quickly retreated to their spots, as if the sidewalk constituted a boundary between volunteers and those experiencing homelessness. Despite the group's emphasis on fellowship and human connection with the people experiencing homelessness, most of the conversation seemed to be taking place between volunteers. The dynamic contrasted sharply with that of majority-white camps and gathering spots.

My interviewees rarely acknowledged this discrepancy. When I asked them point-blank whether race and/or racism might affect volunteer interactions, most color-blind volunteers resisted the idea, with contrived and awkward exchanges often following. The exception was Claire, a member of Fellowship Outreach, who said,

> Sadly, it seems like white volunteers tend to get along the best with white homeless people. And it's like a subconscious thing. But that has only happened one time—in terms of any kind of like outward conflict—and it was during, I think it was [around the time of the August 2014] Ferguson [shooting]. And so, to see other people not being that way, to the degree that I saw and heard from people, it was like "Wow." I mean, it's not like, it's not like Jews in Nazi Germany or anything, but it's there. . . .
>
> Honestly, I don't think it's a prejudice thing, I think it's a culture thing. It's just easier for people of the same culture to interact because they understand each other. . . . It's just you can communicate the most easily with people that you understand culturally. But it's so sad. I mean, it's never ever blatant. Nobody's ever ignored or anything. But it's interesting to me, because like I say, I tend to be drawn to people who are different. So that's been something that I really enjoy about the outreach, is being able to relate to people of all groups. But it's interesting. . . .
>
> I'm really not a normal white person. I'm really not. I love being really down to earth. I'm very, very expressive. And so to me, when I get to relate to Black people, it's like I get to be more myself, because I get to be really, really honest. And so it feels very natural, and it's very fun. And then they receive that. You sense

that whenever you're connecting with somebody. Black people make fun of white people a lot because we're really boring, really nonexpressive, and so when you're expressive and everything, it's just fun.

Despite her willingness to concede this point, Claire kept to the color-blind rule book, attributing difference in interaction and service to culture rather than prejudice. Racial Otherness and implicit biases acted as a barrier to full engagement and personal connection, the primary objective of groups like Fellowship and Right Choice, and I increasingly noticed these differences as my research progressed.

Volunteers entered their work as outreachers with deeply seated beliefs about what race means, and these meanings informed the way they interacted with the world around them. Volunteers' level of comfort around white men, even those who persistently experienced homelessness, meant that they were seen as redeemable. The moral construction of Black urban poverty sets the urban poor outside the class system (Katz 1993; Kelley 1997), but these volunteers believed that some (generally white) people experiencing homelessness could be remade as "productive citizens" through volunteer influence. Although white people experiencing homelessness were marked by their poverty and perceived moral difference (Dunn 2018), race worked in conjunction with class status to inform color-blind volunteers' understandings of urban poverty and service interactions even as the volunteers made contrary claims.

Group members' affinity for whites resulted in stratified services and significant differences in the distribution of supplies between white and Black people experiencing homelessness. As Bolger (2021) has argued, when social service agencies or volunteer groups begin to assign socially constructed labels to different places around the city (e.g., dangerous, friendly, deserving), resources can be unequally distributed and racial disparities perpetuated.

Individuals experiencing homelessness who received frequent visits from Fellowship and Right Choice members—those who had a better connection— seemed to be more comfortable requesting specific supplies. I regularly observed that tents, propane canisters in the winter, and frozen jugs of water in the summer were earmarked for specific people thought to be close with members of the groups. Right Choice even provided a prepaid cell phone to Stan, a white man, although John regularly claimed that he would not do so for others. Although Right Choice developed and maintained a relationship with a small group of Black men on the North Side, the group would also often skip majority-Black gathering spaces and was generally unwilling to go to the North Side after dark. Volunteers regularly worried that predominantly-Black downtown gathering spots would sap their resources without much one-on-one engagement.

CHAPTER 3

"How Do You Relate to Something You Don't Know About?"

Excerpt of an Interview with Christina
Formerly Homeless Black Volunteer with Mercy House
April 10, 2018

Matt (Interviewer): Do you think that race ever matters in the way that interactions play out between service recipients and volunteers?

Christina: Of course it does. It does. It takes us back to the whole, if you don't know, you don't know. When I'm saying that, I'm saying, "How do you relate to something you don't know about?" You don't even know to relate to it in some cases. In some cases, you are closed off to that relation. . . . [African Americans are overrepresented among individuals experiencing homelessness, and] if you did those same quotes or numbers on unemployment, you're going to find the same thing. We're supposed to be such a small number, but we are the biggest number in most of, all of that. So that question—c'mon. Stop it.

(The Limits of) Social and Racial Justice

White Invisibility among Color-Conscious Volunteers

During nights of service, passersby could easily identify Fam in the Streets because at least a few of its members could be counted on to wear their yellow-and-black branded T-shirts as they caravanned around St. Louis providing hot meals in Styrofoam containers. More interesting than the group logo and name on the front was the quote on the back: "Yes, all lives matter, but until mine matters as much as yours, I'm gonna be specific." The predominantly white members of the group commonly cited the quote, attributed to Mama Germaine, a charismatic middle-aged Black woman who served as the undisputed leader of Fam in the Streets. Group members conceptualized their service to St. Louis's homeless population as a form of activism. In fact, many of the longer-term members of Fam in the Streets had met through the 2014 Ferguson protests, and many of the current members belonged to other activist organizations, especially racial justice and antiracist organizations. Most important, they followed Mama Germaine's lead in recognizing inequality as a product of overlapping systems of oppression—in this case, race and class. For her and Fam in the Streets, it followed that service to the unhoused was an act of community and community-building. As she explained to a group of Girl Scouts visiting the group's kitchen on the afternoon of December 14, 2017, 95 percent of people experiencing homelessness in St. Louis are Black, so outreach was "lov[ing] my community."[1]

Although not all volunteers I observed were willing to directly engage with conversations about systemic racism and structural inequalities, this discourse was common among members of Fam in the Streets, Citywide Outreach, Mercy House, and Service House. While all these groups comprised predominantly white volunteers, their color-consciousness should not be seen as surprising. Americans are becoming increasingly aware of structural racial disadvantages, especially Black disadvantage. In fact, when asked which factors were important in explaining Black disadvantage, 80 percent of Americans identified prejudice and discrimination, 45 percent identified laws and institutions, and 85 percent identified schools and social connections (Croll 2013).[2] With antiracist discourse becoming more common among white Americans, it is necessary to consider how well-intentioned, explicitly color-conscious whites understand racialized social problems, race itself, and especially their own whiteness—a task made all the more important given sociology's tendency to favor the study of "marked" categories (Brekhus 1998).[3] While a number of scholars have suggested that regular contact with racialized Others is associated with heightened color-consciousness, improved racial attitudes, and/or antiracist ideologies among whites (Allport 1954; Gallagher 1995, 1997; Hartigan 1997; McDermott 2006; Schneider 2018; Warren 2010), this chapter showcases the limited depth of such consciousness. Specifically, to what degree—if at all—do whites interested in undermining systems of oppression and privilege understand their own place within those systems? The openly color-conscious volunteers framed homelessness and poverty as symptoms of systemic racism, yet notions and consequences of their own whiteness remained underexplored. Conceptualization of Blackness was an ideological tool that could be used to understand a world rife with social and economic inequality. Their own whiteness, conversely, was less salient. Even if on an intellectual level they recognized whiteness as a form of privilege, reflecting on how such privilege informed their motivations, practices, and interactions proved difficult for most volunteers. In fact, when directly asked how their race might inform their interactions with people of color experiencing homelessness, these volunteers were often quick to admit that it must play a role but also were unable to say exactly how it did so or provide examples. Others acknowledged their whiteness in passing—that is, as a characteristic to be suppressed or managed.

Thus, this chapter highlights enduring patterns of white invisibility, even among those who openly contemplate and (attempt to) address problems of racial inequality, racism, and white supremacy. This inability to discuss interracial interactions despite service experiences speaks to the pervasive power and privilege embedded in the taken-for-granted nature of whiteness (Doane 1997; Lipsitz 1998; P. McIntosh 1989) and provides empirical support to the idea that racialized social systems discourage racial self-awareness among whites (Lewis 2004).

Although volunteers displayed strong knowledge of structural racism and/or an-tiracism literature, most understood their own whiteness as a personal trait that could be managed away or neutralized rather than as a structural position. Despite their recognition of oppressive systems, they continue to hold privileged positions within those systems.

This chapter highlights the blind spots among whites who have "done every-thing right." White allyship and color-conscious service to the community must be understood as a continuous process of decolonization and critical reflection. White allyship and color-consciousness is not, as it is often conceptualized, an en-lightened state or individual process (Ray 2020). As such, these white volunteers represent varying points along a spectrum of racial reflexivity, with different stages of recognizing, grappling with, and responding to the realities of racial inequality.

White Invisibility?

Cultural and institutional investments in whiteness mean that white identities, privileges, power, and social patterns are commonly perceived as invisible to the white mainstream (Doane 1997; Du Bois 2015; Lipsitz 1995; P. McIntosh 1989; Rodriguez and Villaverde 2000). Because whiteness has historically been (and re-mains) part and parcel of institutional and cultural power in the United States, patterned white practices, ideologies, beliefs, and the like are framed as norma-tive. In contrast, cultural products and practices of nonwhite minority groups have been Otherized and/or seen as deviant (Doane 1997). "As the unmarked category against which difference is constructed, whiteness never has to speak its name, never has to acknowledge its role as an organizing principle in social and cultural relations" (Lipsitz 1998, 1). Generally speaking, whites are less likely to ac-knowledge the privileges of whiteness and more likely to see the world through an individualistic, color-blind lens than are people of color (Croll 2013; Hartmann, Gerteis, and Croll 2009; Mueller 2017). This white invisibility has had wide-ranging implications for American society. Because whiteness is reproduced as de-fault Americanness, institutional practices said to serve American or community interests are in truth designed to serve white interests (e.g., federal Indian policy, mass incarceration) (Doane 1997; Hernández 2017). Furthermore, public space is better understood as white space: people of color must learn to navigate physical and cultural geographies of white dominance (E. Anderson 2015) as mainstream media simultaneously reproduce unquestioned understandings of whiteness as so-cially and culturally superior (Hughey 2014; Vera and Gordon 2003).

However, many observers have argued that whites are cognizant racial actors. Even if their socialization into American society is not framed in explicitly racial terms, whites interpret social and cultural messages in ways that suggest an understanding of their advanced social position (Hagerman 2018). In fact, the notion of white invisibility has been consistently complicated, if not outright challenged, by scholars since the 1990s. Ruth Frankenberg, who was among the first and most notable whiteness scholars to advance the invisibility thesis, points out that while the power and privileges of whiteness are selectively masked, whiteness periodically marks its difference as necessary to protect its dominant status (Frankenberg 1993, 2001). Others draw attention to whites' tendency to become more cognizant of their racial identity when interacting in predominantly nonwhite spaces (Gallagher 1995, 1997; Schneider 2018). In settings where whites are forced to confront their racial privilege, inequalities are commonly explained away through warped understandings of individual achievement and cultural difference and/or by minimizing and naturalizing racial disparities (Bonilla-Silva 2010; Croll 2013; DiTomaso, Parks-Yancy, and Post 2003).

The salience of racial inequality and white privilege is not always easy to ignore. With challenges to white privilege growing in strength and frequency in the United States, many whites are learning to manage their racial identity in a way that acknowledges the past and current oppression of people of color (Beeman 2022; Hughey 2007; Knowles et al. 2014). While many whites continue to deny the existence of racial privilege and distance themselves from privileged self-concepts, acknowledging racial inequality and working to dismantle systems that produce racial inequality has also emerged as a way of managing white identities and senses of self (Knowles et al. 2014). And although whites are typically seen as more likely to deny or distance (Knowles et al. 2014), a growing body of literature is dedicated to understanding those interested in dismantling racist systems of oppression (Appiah and Gutmann 1996; Feagin and O'Brien 2004; Hughey 2007; Kendi 2019; O'Brien 2001; Tochluk 2010; Warren 2010).

White Antiracism and Color-Conscious Service

Antiracism, broadly speaking, is any ideology or practice meant to challenge racism. Education scholars Robert D. Reason and Nancy J. Evans (2007) have noted that for whites, awareness of one's whiteness is a prerequisite to engaging in racial justice work. However, being "antiracist," an "ally," or "woke" looks vastly different depending on the accompanying understanding of racism and antiracism (Hage 2016; O'Brien 2009; Paradies 2016). Because the United States remains racially segregated, both physically and socially (Crowder 2000; Crowder and South 2008; Hagerman 2018; May 2014), some scholars have suggested that many whites may have only a limited ability to adopt color-conscious, antiracist ideologies and practices (Brown 2017; Feagin and O'Brien 2004; Mueller and Washington 2021; Warren 2010). In turn, scholars frequently discuss white antiracism in terms of discovery (Case 2012; Helms 1997; O'Brien and Korgen 2007; Perry and Shotwell 2009; Thompson 2001; Warren 2010). In this view, "moral shock" leads whites to develop a more salient white identity as they question their own position and make connections with people of other racial groups. Such relationships are then credited with leading white antiracists to understand their relative privilege (Helms 1997; Warren 2010). Following the basic premise provided by Gordon Allport's (1954) contact hypothesis, this theory commonly credits interracial friendships as the impetus for antiracist advocacy, although some scholarship has suggested that color-blind ideology prevents many whites from having meaningful interactions with people of color about racism and that many whites are introduced to antiracism through white friends; environments that encourage reflection on questions of race, racism, and whiteness; or social support systems (Feagin and O'Brien 2004; Fingerhut and Hardy 2020; O'Brien and Korgen 2007; Reason and Evans 2007; Thompson 2001).

Progressive interpretations of antiracism view race as a social construction and accept racism as real and as embedded in social systems and practices. As George J. Sefa Dei (1996, 254) explains, critical antiracism "moves beyond acknowledgement of the material conditions that structure societal inequality to question white power and privilege and its accompanying rationale for dominance." Thus, in principle, antiracism serves a range of functions, including "reducing the incidence of racist practices," "fostering a non-racist culture," "supporting the victims of racism," "empowering racialized subjects," "transforming racist relations into better relations," and "fostering an a-racist culture" (Hage 2016, 124).

The heavy structural and cultural investment in whiteness, however, means that all whites identifying as antiracists are not equally prepared for antiracist praxis. By definition, antiracists must be willing to acknowledge to some degree the importance of race and persistence of racism/racial inequalities (Appiah and Gutmann 1996), but that degree varies. Frankenberg (1993, 157), for example, details how "race cognizance" among white women in California was commonly associated with antiracist discourse and political action. Likewise, Michael Omi's (2001) inventory of antiracist organizations in the United States shows that institutionalized and intersectional understandings of racism and other systems of oppression are common.

Even so, scholars such as Matthew W. Hughey (2007, 2010) and Alastair Bonnett (1996) demonstrate that white antiracists are prone to essentializing race, viewing "white" as fixed and monolithic. Eileen O'Brien (2001), Angie Beeman (2022), and Shannon Sullivan (2014) call attention to limitations of "selective race

cognizance" and the classed moral distancing performed by politically progressive and "good" middle-class white people. Even race-cognizant, antiracist whites
struggle to be reflexive. For whites confronted by such challenges, white privilege
can be understood in the abstract and as something reproduced by social institutions even as they struggle to recognize how social forces affect them as individuals—how they personally benefit from white privilege. At the same time, allyship
efforts routinely propose individualized solutions to systemic inequality rather
than considering and approaching such problems from a structural vantage point
(Sumerau et al. 2021). Thus, even as U.S. whites increasingly profess interest in antiracism and diversity, there is no guarantee that this interest will lead to greater
racial equity or that whites will develop an effective antiracist praxis. For that result to occur, according to philosophers Pamela Perry and Alexis Shotwell (2009),
whites must develop a "relational understanding" of racism. Antiracist consciousness and practice necessitate propositional, tacit, and affective forms of knowledge. Whites must recognize that social and cultural systems convey privileges to
those racialized as white, that they as individuals are situated within these systems,
and that they are connected to others (often understood through emotions like
empathy).

Considering that participants in formal volunteer activities are likely to be
white (Bortree and Waters 2014; Foster-Bey 2008; Gonzales et al. 2016; Rotolo,
Wilson, and Hughes 2010) and to come from middle-income homes (Foster-Bey
2008; Gonzales et al. 2016; Y. Lee and Brudney 2009; Pho 2008), volunteers and
other service providers present an important case for critical study. Although volunteering is commonly thought of in altruistic terms and is best defined as helping
activities engaged in without expectation of reward (Snyder and Omoto 2008),
scholars of race and community engagement have begun to question the role and
impact of volunteers. If whites are merely rational actors interested in the preserv-
ing systems of oppression and privilege, it would seem strange that volunteer organizations are disproportionately comprised of people with privileged racial, class,
and education statuses (Foster-Bey 2008). While the emphasis on helping in defi-
nitions of volunteering may have more to do with framing than with the motivations or the actual impact of volunteering, juxtaposing volunteering with whiteness in this way seemingly presents a contradiction. In turn, some observers have
pointed out the ways in which volunteering reifies difference and/or inequality.

Scholars have begun to pay particularly close attention to the ways whiteness
operates in volunteer, activist, and service learning settings (e.g., Droogendyk
et al. 2016; Endres and Gould 2009; Germann Molz 2017; J. Henry 2022; Schneider 2018). Whiteness has been found to significantly inform volunteer goals, interactions, and perceptions (Germann Molz 2017; J. Henry 2022; Kipp, Hawkins,

and Gray 2021; Lough and Carter-Black 2015; Schneider 2018). Danielle Endres and Mary Gould (2009, 429), for example, find that service learning students who have been exposed to critical whiteness studies routinely centered their individual experiences and justified "white privilege as a way to provide charity." Sociologist Margaret A. Hagerman (2018, 140) shows that explicitly color-conscious white parents interested in teaching their children about privilege sometimes expose their children to racial and economic inequality through local and international volunteer work: "Without a doubt, the kids in this study learn a great deal from both volunteering and vacationing, including many positive lessons about community, ethical responsibility, and the reality of inequality. However, one of the lessons they also learn is that they can navigate the world fluidly and with ease without ever asking for permission, a hallmark of privilege."

And while volunteering comes with numerous benefits for volunteers, including career-related experience, life experience, social capital, and a chance to develop useful or marketable skills (Cann and McCloskey 2017; Clary and Snyder 1999; Eliasoph 2013; Germann Molz 2017; Putnam 2000; Skocpol 1997, 1999), volunteer programs may offer limited benefits or even negative outcomes for service recipients (Blouin and Perry 2009; Cann and McCloskey 2017; Lasker 2016). In fact, service-learning programs that place underprepared students in community organizations can drain the organization's time and resources. When volunteers lack necessary skills, organizations may shift focus away from the service population and toward training (often short-term) volunteers (Blouin and Perry 2009). A case study by Colette N. Cann and Erin McCloskey (2017) examines a historically white college's tutoring outreach program that places well-intentioned but underprepared students in a low-income, predominantly nonwhite middle school. While the university leveraged this program for significant grant money and college tutors gained valuable experience, the benefit to the middle school and its students was questionable. Such projects reproduce narratives of white saviorhood without undermining "issues of institutional and systemic racism that keep Schools of Color and their communities subordinated" (82; see also Droogendyk et al. 2016; Endres and Gould 2009; Hanchey 2018).

Despite volunteers' positive intentions, their actions do not exist in a vacuum. Volunteering is practiced in a social world shaped by whiteness in which it "goes unnoticed" because whites "are not oriented 'towards' it" (Ahmed 2007, 156). Thus, volunteering operations must be subject to critical examination, including how social and cultural investments in whiteness shape the ways white volunteers frame inequality, service, and activism.

Justice: Volunteer Understandings of Race, Racism, and Inequality in St. Louis

It became clear early in my fieldwork that volunteers providing grassroots home-less services approached this work with two general understandings of homeless-ness. One view leaned heavily on "commonsense" notions of poverty: homeless-ness resulted from individual choices or (lack of) effort, and issues of race and racism were rarely if ever featured in dialogue. The second view perceived home-lessness as the product of institutional barriers and arrangements and saw it as deeply intertwined with understandings of race and racism. Rather than suggest that people experiencing homelessness pull themselves up by their bootstraps, pro-ponents of this view pointed to long-standing issues of systemic racism and sought to have the St. Louis city government better protect the rights of citizens experi-encing homelessness and provide infrastructure to support safety and social mo-bility (e.g., more temporary shelter beds, day centers, permanent shelter, and reha-bilitation services).

Many volunteers expressed these abstract ideas through the language of social justice. According to Joseph, a retired white man heavily involved in the provision of transitional and (semi)permanent shelter through Citywide, a commitment to social justice means a commitment

> to trying to change the conditions. Not just to be charitable and give money to the poor or whatever, but try to change the systems that cause poverty, that cause discrimination, that cause racial injustice, that cause a lack of affordable housing. I was a developer. My first job was as a consultant. I was a real estate consultant for nine years, and then I went to work as a director of the first redevelopment corporation around Washington New Medical Center. And one of my main jobs was to get rid of all the boardinghouses and rooming houses along West Pine and Laclede, which were a problem. But I look back on that now and think, "Well, yeah, I was getting rid of some problems, but I was also getting rid of a lot of af-fordable housing." And I feel like it's karma for me to be creating affordable hous-ing now—very affordable, because I certainly was responsible for getting rid of some of it earlier. So that's what I mean by social justice is not just charitable giv-ing but changing the system.

The source of Joseph's reflexive hindsight is unclear, and he was exceptional in that he viewed his current volunteer work as a sort of penance for his earlier role in the gentrification of the Central West End neighborhood. However, his view of in-equality was far from exceptional. He and other "woke" volunteers framed their work as (attempting to be) transformational and social-justice-oriented because the goal was to change the system so that people in poverty could simply access housing. Homelessness and poverty, in this view, are (re)produced and exacerbated through social policy, markets, and other social institutions. Thus, any approach to abating homelessness needs to consider changes or alternatives to existing institutions and/or systems of oppression. Joseph included race as one of these systems of injustice, tying it to economic inequality and access to affordable housing.

Likewise, René, a white therapist/social worker who was in her first year of service with Citywide Outreach, believed that the United States and St. Louis in particular needed a "cultural shift" toward understanding poverty as a structural outcome rather than as a personal trouble (Mills 2000):

> I think we need a major cultural shift, because other developed countries don't have this kind of problem that we do. . . . I think our society is very individualistic, and I think that we see other people's problems as not really our problems. And "That's on them," and "I'm going to worry about me," and "I've worked hard for my shit, sorry," "I've worked hard for what I have, and if you didn't"—because that's the perception—"if you didn't, that's kind of on you," and "If I'm okay, I'm okay with that, that's okay, that's enough." . . . I feel like, society can all do better if everyone had their basic needs met in terms of the economy and the health and happiness of our society.

In René's view, systems of (un)housing are upheld and justified by flawed cultural logics, ideologies, and practices, and she pointed to a problem caused by abstracting the principles of liberalism (see Bonilla-Silva 2010) to frame homelessness and poverty as an individual problem. In addition, she asserted that this cultural ideology frames the world in a way that is detrimental to societal health, happiness, and economy. René also understood systems of privilege and oppression, especially race, as important predictors of social and material outcomes:

> A vast majority of the people I see who are homeless are Black, are people of color. Those are the people who have a lack of resources or access to resources. Our whole city is set up like that. The whole [predominantly Black] north part of this city is without a public hospital and very many grocery stores and a lot of nonprofit agencies like the one I work at that would help people with meeting their basic needs. There just aren't that many of them up there. [There isn't] good public transportation. . . .
>
> I think [race] ties into the equation; I think it might be like one of the biggest if not the [biggest] contributing factor to someone being homeless. You're just more likely to be homeless if you're a person of color. You're just more likely to ex-

perience the things that lead to homelessness. Simple as that. I think it's the over-arching factor that someone experiences. . . . By setting up all these barriers for people of color that we have in this city, pushing them all to one side of the city and leaving that area without any resources, we're just asking for this epidemic here.

Such understandings of poverty and homelessness were common among antirac-ist, social-justice-oriented volunteers. Understanding homelessness and poverty meant understanding overlapping social institutions and systems of oppression. For these volunteers, understanding poverty meant also considering problems of race, social welfare, policing, and government policy. Homelessness and poverty, in their view, are reproduced and exacerbated through social policy, markets, and other social institutions. Thus, any remedy to homelessness needs to consider al-ternatives to existing institutions and/or systems of oppression. For these volun-teers, anti-Black racism was a particularly important tool that allowed them to understand uneven access to social, economic, and political resources (Omi and Winant 1994).

Volunteers often cited the need for specific policy measures, such as a home-less bill of rights or the reestablishment of day centers. At other times, volun-teers called for a full-scale revolution. Invoking the words of Catholic social ac-tivist Dorothy Day, some Catholic Workers were fond of saying that they were attempting to "build a new world in the shell of the old."[4] Others, like Thomas (white) and Cecilia (Black), a young couple, talked at length about the need for a communist revolution, tying problems of homelessness and racism to the ex-ploitive capitalist system.

To their credit, color-conscious white volunteers frequently considered the role of racism in structuring community relations and how they as relatively privileged community members could respond to these problems. Justin, a white recent col-lege graduate who spent a year living at and working through Service House, ex-plained that his roommates (five white, one Black) regularly discussed how to un-derstand race in a time of racial reckoning:

> When most people come into a different area, they would look at it as, "Oh, we're these figures to *help*." Or "This is a charity case. Yeah. We're about to do so much good." [My roommates] don't look at it like that, and that's what I love about my roommates: the humility that everyone displays here. There's very little if no hubris at all. I don't sense this air of, "Oh, I'm elite. I'm helping out these underprivileged areas." It's very much, "So I want to be a part of this commu-nity." That's assuring, knowing that the events of Ferguson, etc., all of these things that were happening in St. Louis to re-spark national debate, it's, "Do we live in a

postracial society? Is gentrification really a thing? Is white flight really a thing? Is police brutality really a thing?" They get it. And they're willing to have those difficult conversations as well, and [they're] peeling back their own layers of blindness, and so am I. I realize so much more about my own blind spots. We're all aware that we have blind spots that we need to work on and things that we need working on internally as well.

Although conversations among volunteers of similarly privileged social positions may well lack necessary perspectives and lay volunteers are not always well equipped to have well-rounded and productive conversations about racism and poverty in North St. Louis, many volunteers showed genuine interest in understanding racial injustice. Like Justin, many volunteers credited the murder of Michael Brown and the ensuing protests as spurring such conversations. How Justin came to understand racial justice as important is not clear, but Brown's murder seems to have represented a moment of "moral shock," causing Justin and others to realize that police brutality (not only against Brown but also against racial justice protesters) did not fit with their values systems (Warren 2010). Further, Justin, Joseph, and others may have had networks that exposed them to antiracist ideologies (Feagin and O'Brien 2004; O'Brien and Korgen 2007). Regardless of the impetus, Justin's disposition toward antiracist ideals was an ongoing project through his involvement with Service House. Justin might represent an entry point to antiracism. He had begun openly to grapple with racial inequality and through Service House was engaged in work that he hoped would undermine that inequality. His conversations with his roommates reinforced and molded his view of the world as a social product of competing racist social systems and affirmed his desire to serve marginalized communities. In fact, this phenomenon was a staple across volunteer groups.

In addition to providing a common goal, groups provided volunteers with a support network to which they could turn as they worked through their understandings of inequality. Volunteers relied on their peers to continue the learning process. For example, Barbara, a middle-aged white woman who spent more than twenty years in service to Mercy House, explained that she was always challenging herself to continue her antiracist education by engaging with a variety of volunteer, activist, and antiracist groups. She noted that Mercy House had recently put out a newsletter on the subject of gentrification and how

all that is related to colonialism. So [I now understand] that a little bit better. And I am not an expert. I have a lot of learning to do about that specifically. For myself, I've learned just a lot about oppression in the last five years and have gotten extra training, and I'm working with other groups that do education on oppression, antioppression work, and that has been pretty life-changing and has helped me see people's different identities in the way that people have unearned privilege, but the way that they're targeted in that and that kind of thing. So that has been really helpful to put things into context, I think. . . .

The other group I work with is called the Community Justice Collective–St. Louis, and they do diversity and inclusion work in St. Louis from a very Paulo Freire, deep social change, systemic analysis kind of perspective. So that has been really powerful. . . . Understanding that I have targeted identities [helps] me understand that I work here, and when I compare myself to women who live here—I am a white person, I'm a middle-class person, and I'm an agent [whereas] they are targeted. And also I'm a lesbian, so I am targeted in that identity in a way that straight people aren't, and so understanding that mosaic, that we're all a mix of those things. It's just important to consider all of them, and just because I'm white doesn't mean that I'm not targeted with my sexual orientation or being a woman and that kind of thing. Learning that both/and concept has been really really helpful—that you can just hold a lot of simultaneous truths.

Barbara's experiences have led her to develop an understanding of inequality that is in line with the principles of intersectionality (Browne and Misra 2003; Collins 2000, 2013; Crenshaw 1991). Barbara also suggests, perhaps unintentionally, that in her everyday work, her statuses as white and middle-class exist in relation to the targeted identities of those she serves at Mercy House.

Participating in this sort of group discourse was productive, especially when groups were making a conscious effort to critically engage with concepts such as intersectionality and social justice alongside Freire and others. But although the interest in social justice and systemic inequality provided the ideological grounding for these antiracist volunteer groups, volunteers only rarely reflected on how their statuses of privilege (especially their white middle-classness) might impact their day-to-day service interactions.

Seeing White Privilege in Social Structure, Not as Everyday Power Relations

Whiteness is often unquestioned or viewed "as an unimportant *individual* attribute rather than a defining feature of a white *group* identity" (Underhill 2019, 493; see also Doane 1997; Lewis 2004). And although the true invisibility of white racial identities has been rightfully questioned—whites can be aware racial actors (Frankenberg 2001; Hartigan 1999; Knowles et al. 2014; McDermott 2006; McDermott and Samson 2005)—volunteers showed time and again that even those who talk about whiteness and white privilege in the abstract are unlikely to think about the effects of whiteness on their everyday interactions. Although many volunteers understood the structural constraints and advantages endemic to white supremacist society, they neglected to consider how they, as members of the white racial group, were enmeshed in system of power relations that informed and affected their interactions and relationships with both white and nonwhite people experiencing homelessness.

Openly color-conscious volunteers, many of whom identified as antiracist activists, commonly expressed a sense of surprise when explicitly asked about how race might affect their service interactions. Gabriela, a white retired social worker who regularly volunteered with Citywide, responded to that question with "Oh, that's a good one!" and then paused before continuing:

> I don't know. I want to say, "No, we've all got the great big liberal hearts." But you know what, I don't know. I would hope that if [race was a factor] that I'd become aware of it and be able to address that. But I'll tell you what, since Michael Brown, here in the St. Louis region, I have personally become so much more aware and educated about the racism that goes on in my life and in this community. God, I just hope that I can be aware if that's an issue. I don't feel like it is, but you know what, if somebody said, "Gabriela, you act differently here than you do here," I would want to know that. Because so often I just am reacting to stuff and doing stuff that I don't see it, but I would hope that somebody—and I'll tell you, some of those activist volunteers, especially with Fam in the Streets, they would be happy to point it out, I know they would—in a good way, in a kind way—to point out that they saw some volunteers showing some kind of difference between people, in colored people and people that are white. And I think they would. I would hope I would be able to. But you know what? What I'm aware of is how much I'm not aware of.

Gabriela had not previously reflected on how race might inform service interactions, though she was willing to admit that it might. In this way, white, explicitly color-conscious volunteers walked a middle ground between understanding whiteness as a group position laden with structural advantages and whiteness as an individual characteristic. Whereas Justin was openly grappling with the existence of racial inequality but only beginning to question the extent to which racism threads through American social institutions, Gabriela was questioning the extent to which her whiteness had shaped her perceptions.

In a social world where racial inequality and racism are increasingly salient, particularly in St. Louis, where racial injustice protest is common, Joseph, René, Barbara, Justin, Gabriela, and other volunteers became aware and worked to educate themselves on the subject in the abstract. Identifying as antiracists interested in dismantling racist systems of oppression likely helped them manage their self-images at a time when white privilege was more frequently being questioned (Knowles et al. 2014). However, the cultural, social, political, and institutional investment in whiteness (Doane 1997; Lipsitz 1998) prevented volunteers from applying that framework to their own lives. As Paul, a Mercy House volunteer, succinctly put it, "I'm white, and things like that don't really stick out to me because I don't know what's racist and what's not. So I'm sure that I've done many things that were problematic, but I don't know."

This is not to say that openly color-conscious volunteers were uninterested in trying to manage their whiteness. Rather, their ability to know what to manage had limitations. For Paul and Joan, only their relationships with Julia, a Filipinx peer, gave meaning to their whiteness in their everyday lives. Joan, a white core community member at Mercy House, recounted the stimulus for deeper reflection on her everyday service interactions:

> Paul and I actually have weekly meetings now to specifically talk about our own racism and the racism in the house, and I'm really pleased that we're doing that. So this isn't to say that [our racism is] not still a focus, but the impetus for those meetings was a particular hot period with these issues about a month ago, where Julia got just kind of fed up with these two privileged young white kids oblivious to their racism in a lot of ways, and her having to deal with the consequences of that was just exhausting.
>
> What struck me the most about those conversations was just how much rage Julia had and how much she had sheltered us from that. I don't want to for a moment perpetuate the story of the angry woman of color—her rage was justified. The weariness and the exhaustion she must have been feeling—I would have been pissed too. It was just realizing in that moment how difficult it was for her as a person of color in core community and how difficult it must have been for every other person of color who's been in core community. That's sort of what struck me the most, just how much weariness and how much justified anger the white people in this community have been sheltered from, in large part because nobody wants to deal with the level of defensiveness and/or guilt that arises when white people—especially young, relatively sheltered white people—are called out on their racism like that. It made me realize just how omnipresent racism must feel to at the very least people of color in core community but also probably to a lot of our guests and just how invisible it can be to the white people in the house if you aren't making an effort to look for—and even when you are—that

divide. It really surprised me, and having that happen within our core community made me wonder how old of a story that really is. For how many years have the white people here been protected from the worst of the outrage that they generate, of the pain that they cause?

White volunteers' failure to consider their own whiteness was both the outcome of and tool for the reproduction of day-to-day power relations that Joan believed profoundly affected those they encountered as well as on white volunteers' ability to serve a majority-Black population. Only after an intervention by Julia, a uniquely qualified volunteer of color with a background in antiracist activism and community organizing, were Paul and Joan moved to begin reflecting on their implicitly racist behaviors.

Although Paul and Joan also seem to recognize the ongoing nature of antiracism, they continue to view their whiteness as something to be unpacked and then shed (P. McIntosh 1989; Omi 2001). Yet Joan also recognized the omnipresence of racism. It is a normal part of everyday life in the United States, embedded into both microlevel relations and social institutions (Aviles de Bradley 2015; Christian 2019; Christian, Seamster, and Ray 2019; Delgado and Stefancic 2012; Ray 2019; Rosino 2017) and affecting everyone, white and nonwhite (Lewis 2004). Whites must situate themselves within broader systems of oppression and privilege especially if they hope to undermine them (Perry and Shotwell 2009). Thus, many white volunteers' continued inability to understand their day-to-day interactions as the product of unequal group positions may limit the effectiveness of supposedly color-conscious service.

Toward Volunteer Understandings of Privilege and Group Position

A common critique holds that whites' antiracist efforts to unpack their privilege end up centering whiteness and consequently marginalizing issues of racism and the lived experiences of people of color (Hughey 2007, 2012; Kowal 2015; Mayorga-Gallo 2019; Omi 2001). Positions of privilege must be understood in relation to positions of oppression. Whiteness is defined by its position relative to Blackness, Latinxness, and so forth (Blumer 1958; Lipsitz 1998; Omi 2001; Winant 2004). Homelessness is defined in relation to being housed (Willse 2015). Service provider/volunteer status is defined in relation to service recipient.

René similarly suggested that her whiteness could be managed in her interactions with Black service recipients either as a volunteer or as a professional social worker:

It's something I think about all the time in terms of just kind of check my privilege and feeling like not walking into someone's space like I own the place. I don't
want to ever come across as an authority or a white savior or anything like that.
It's something I'm thinking about a lot. I hope it doesn't come across. It's something I'm always very cognizant of.

René implicitly acknowledged that she occupies a position of power but nevertheless dismissed the idea that her structural position mattered. Instead, she suggested
that she could shed her position of authority by being cognizant of the way she
enters space. Despite being white and housed, she understood that social institutions ranging from government to private business were integral to reproducing
social inequality. Nevertheless, when entering into interpersonal interactions, she
dismissed her statuses of privilege as manageable, as an inconsequential personal
trait, rather than as a position structured in dominance four hundred years in the
making (Frankenberg 2001; Underhill 2019; Winant 2004).

All groups symbolically attempted to flatten hierarchical power structures by
situating people experiencing homelessness as equal-status peers. Members of Fam
in the Streets referred to people experiencing homelessness as "Fam," "Family,"
or "unhoused brothers and sisters." Members of many other groups spoke about
people experiencing homelessness as unhoused or homeless "friends." One white
Citywide volunteer, Tatiana, explained that she enjoyed collecting stories from
"sojourners" in an effort to find commonalities with them. These connections
were often as simple as relating on the basis of age or health problems, but she val-
ued the feeling of having something in common with those she served.

Conversely, Barbara poked holes in this kind of thinking, speaking often of a
"false sense of sameness." After many years of service to Mercy House, she had begun to understand that while she can unpack her privilege, she cannot shed it. On
one occasion, Barbara explained that she had spent her twenties trying to achieve
this false sense of sameness by living the "simplest" life possible:

> I feel like that's very much against the spirit of everything. We're trying to do
> collaboration here, and some kind of spitting contest about who can get more
> clothes from the thrift store—it feels like it's a misplaced [emphasis]. It felt like
> a way to be OK—to make myself feel better about all the privilege I had and in
> a way that wasn't actually liberatory in some ways because I wasn't gaining new
> skills in some ways. I don't know that it most of the time created more connec-
> tion. . . .
>
>   And I feel like there's a tremendous amount of white guilt and class, mid-
> dle-class guilt, that I had and wasn't super aware of, but I was trying to do this
> work as sort of reparations for it—"I have to do something with all this privilege."

And I feel like the voluntary poverty, in some ways it's like just part of the fabric, and it's communal living and sharing. But in some ways, it can fall into just a self-righteous distancing thing that creates barriers. So me not having health insurance for the first few years—I was super radical and [acting] like I'm all that about it. But the [service recipients] here were like, "You could have health insurance. What is wrong with you?"

Which, to me, is right. Am I helping them? Am I helping them directly by not having health insurance? No. Am I changing any system by not having health insurance? No. . . . A huge piece of voluntary poverty is not participating in unjust structures, but I think I didn't have a handle on [the idea that] every single structure in this country is built on slavery and capitalism and terrible. And so by walking down the street, I'm participating. And there has to be a more sophisticated way to address it than to try to on an individual level be super-pure and withdraw from everything.

Barbara pointed out that she and the "guests" at Mercy House never were and never could be in the same position. Her class position meant that she would always have a safety net. Despite her largely class-based analysis here, she recognized that her whiteness came with privileges that most guests could not attain, that her status as a volunteer put her in a position of power, and that her class was intimately intertwined with these other status positions. She went on to relate an incident when she was twenty-five years old "and doing a budget with a forty-year-old mother":

The truth is I actually don't have the skills that I think I have. I don't have the resiliency that's born out of struggle, because class-wise, most things have been handed to me. So it's an irony that I'm put in the position of being an authority with somebody who has had to work the system in a way that I am completely unaware of. So it's a really ugly interaction because I have authority over their housing, so they have to modify their responses and their behavior knowing—I mean, they should tell me to fuck off, right? "You don't know what you're talking about. Have you raised [children]?" And I do understand that it's not so simplistic that you have to have experienced every scenario in order to have insight into it, but I think when we have more fallen on the side of things of thinking that because we have privilege, we know better. So budgeting, how you should interact with your kids, what decisions you should make for your kids—so many things that I have thought that I should have known better.

Barbara recognizes the power and privilege bound up in her race and class position, showing an understanding of race and class that most other color-conscious

social-justice-oriented volunteers lacked. She understood that racism and social inequality more generally involve group position, not just social boundaries that can
be crossed when privilege is checked. To be white is to hold power. To be middle-
class is to hold power. To be a volunteer is to hold power. It is more productive
for volunteers to reflect on their social position and to critically interrogate what
actions might work to undermine the unequal systems that placed them in a position of authority.

The volunteers featured in this chapter and in chapter 2 showcased varying levels of racial reflexivity. Barbara demonstrated the most advanced understanding of
whiteness as a system and her place within it. Justin placed more emphasis on recognizing the role social institutions played in the reproduction of racial inequality.
Falling somewhere in between Justin and Barbara, Gabriela, René, Joan, and Paul
represented in various ways that they were grappling with the hard-to-see consequences of their racial group position for their perception.

However, people's positions on the spectrum are not fixed and are likely to
change, in part because of their commitments to antiracism. Moreover, the representation of individual volunteers on a left-to-right diagram cannot be fairly interpreted as any sort of antiracism ranking. What most obviously binds together
the volunteers on the right half of the spectrum is their acknowledgment that they
were actively engaged in a process of (re)learning about race, racial inequality,
and/or racial privilege and oppression. In the words of Victor Ray (2020), "Antiracism is a constant struggle," with no end point.

Representing racial reflexivity on a spectrum implies a fixed or uniform path
through ordered stages. While a progression from a recognition of inequality or
unfairness through a recognition of one's position in oppressive social hierarchies

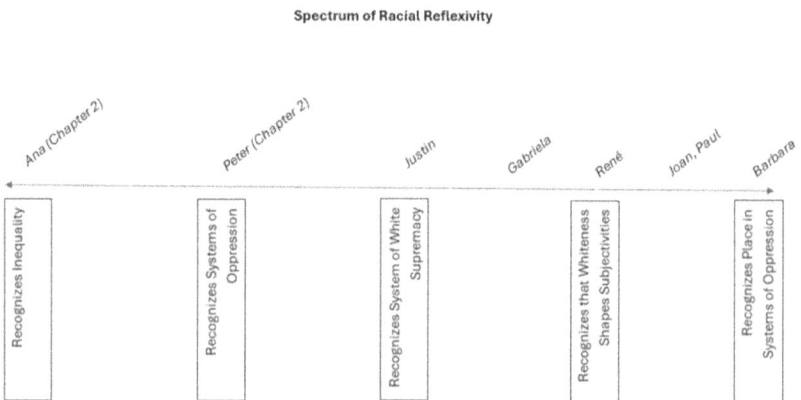

FIGURE 6. The spectrum of racial reflexivity. © Matthew Jerome Schneider.

may roughly track with the experiences of many white antiracists, others may follow a different path, and the process is not likely to be smooth, unidirectional, or ever wholly complete.

Sociologist Wayne Brekhus (1998, 45) has argued for a sociology that "mark[s] everything." "Reverse marking," he writes, "helps to destabilize markedness by compensating against the excessive articulation of the poles; if we articulate entire continua with equal weight, there will be no negative spaces left." This continuum falls well short of marking all social behaviors, attitudes, and identities but nonetheless contributes to Brekhus's larger intellectual project by articulating practiced forms of whiteness. This visual depiction of racial reflexivity highlights that it is not a binary option, with some people being racially reflexive and others not. Instead, it draws attention to many points in between with varying levels of racial reflexivity possible.

CHAPTER 4

"They Get So Creative"

Excerpt from Right Choice Ministry and Outreach Fieldnotes

April 23, 2018

FIGURE 7. An abandoned warehouse on the North Side, with downtown St. Louis visible in the distance, May 30, 2021. © Matthew Jerome Schneider.

The evening of April 23, 2018, like many evenings, featured heavy doses of volunteer photography. In fact, by the time we arrived at Stan's warehouse dwelling, photography had become an openly acknowledged theme of the outing. Over the course of the evening, I had been carpooling with a cheery white volunteer. After parking at the end of the caravan, the volunteer hopped out of my old green CRV and announced that the aging warehouse in which Stan lived would be a great place for a photo shoot. She dramatically leaned up against the wall, indicating the pose she would strike for the camera. She then called to Gregory's daughter and suggested the girl take a photo with the building. The girl did, much to the volunteer's satisfaction.

Meanwhile, John marched up to the warehouse door. He knocked but did not wait for Stan to answer. After just a few brief seconds, he began fumbling with the bottom of the door, eventually managing to slide it halfway open, showing no respect for the place Stan and a couple of others called home. It was treated as a public space that John could access because he was looking for someone. In the months since first meeting Stan, the group's attitude toward him had showed signs of souring. Group members were becoming frustrated that he was still without work, and tonight, John meant business. This was an attitude that resulted when "friends" did not prioritize his regular Monday visits, apparently empowering him to enter Stan's home without permission. He looked in and asked if anyone was there. After a two-second delay, Stan, who was already on his way to the door, called back to greet John.

Once at the door, there were so many people gathered around Stan, who was the only one home today, that I could not properly listen in on the conversation he was having with John. I did manage to hear John ask if anyone had delivered firewood recently. Stan said, "No," but Teresa, who was standing next to me, immediately chimed in to undermine him, announcing that the Thursday group, led by Raymond, had delivered a load of wood last week.

I must not have been the only one who felt unable to participate in the conversation with Stan, because Gregory had turned on his flashlight app and was leaning into the warehouse door, looking for the family of raccoons that shared the warehouse. Right Choice volunteers had been fascinated by the idea of men rooming with the raccoons since they first witnessed them in February.[1] The novelty clearly had not worn off, as Gregory was diligent in his search. When Dominic noticed what was happening, he leaned in behind Gregory and let out a hissing imitation of a raccoon, making Gregory jump back and clutch his chest as the group laughed.

At this point, people began to take more interest in Stan's living arrangement. John began to take photos of the inside. Half joking—but only half—Stan leaned over to John to say, "No photos. No Proof." John persisted anyway, taking more photos as he explained that he likes the light offered by the fire burning across the cluttered warehouse floor. Many of the others leaned in to inspect the warehouse, including Britta, an irregular Black member of the group, who was also taking photos. Pauline, a Black, first-time attendee, added, "They get so creative."

Service as Poverty Tourism?

The Volunteer Gaze and Its Implications

Poverty tourism, also known as slum tourism, is the practice of purposefully "trav-el[ing] to impoverished areas" (Scheyvens 2001, 18), but the term often refers spe-cifically to guided tours through the urban slums of the Global South (Mesch-kank 2011). The practice has become a popular form of development, with the townships of Johannesburg and the favelas of Rio de Janeiro receiving the most traffic (Frenzel et al. 2015). In the American context, homeless outreach volunteer-ing bears a striking similarity to poverty tourism. The privileges and power asso-ciated with volunteer statuses—especially those of being white, housed, and/or middle class—shape perceptions of and interactions in urban spaces racialized as Black. Much like poverty tourism in the Global South, the tourist gaze displayed by volunteers in marginal urban space emphasizes and helps reify their differences, both perceived and material, with those they seek to help. Alongside their interest in meeting the needs of people experiencing homelessness, volunteers ultimately reinforced unhoused people's marginal social positions. Furthermore, the Other-ization process varies based on the ideological bent of the volunteer group. Those who more readily deployed color-conscious racial justice frames fixed their gazes on a consumable Blackness. Meanwhile, those who understood homelessness through the lens of color blindness and individualism cast a gaze that implicitly constructed white homelessness as difference but Black homelessness as danger, a product of laziness, and/or cultural deficiency.

Many observers see poverty tourism as a sustainable alternative that promotes community development (Scheyvens 2001), while others see poverty tourism as voyeuristic (Dovey and King 2012; D. Harrison 2008), leading to disagreements over poverty tourism's proper place in development efforts. Touristic volunteering should not be framed in either/or terms. Volunteers were capable of simultaneously making a tangible impact on disadvantaged members of the St. Louis community and cementing the marginalized position of those experiencing homelessness. Volunteers not only consumed these marginal urban spaces and people but also helped reproduce them as a spectacle of Otherness.

Perceptions of the Other and of Otherized Space

The construction and perception of Black poverty and Black urban space is often problematic. General understandings of homelessness, in contrast, are largely sympathetic (Link et al. 1995; Toro et al. 2007). In contrast to social and political issues such as affirmative action and welfare "dependency," which have been racialized as Black issues, the issue of homelessness—at least in the abstract—is often associated with white men. Although homelessness disproportionately affects Black Americans—although only about 13.4 percent of the U.S. population is African American (U.S. Census Bureau 2018), an estimated 39.1 percent of people experiencing homelessness are Black (M. Henry, Watt, and Shivji 2016)—homelessness is not necessarily perceived as a Black issue. When Americans think of homelessness, they may conjure images of the traveling hobo, "white men, 'enslaved' by poverty" (Higbie 2003, 93). Americans seem to forget, ignore, or fail to realize that children, families, and women account for a significant percentage of the population experiencing homelessness (B. A. Lee, Tyler, and Wright 2010). In George Wilson's (1996) study, Baltimore residents perceived people experiencing homelessness as white, while people dependent on welfare were perceived as Black. In turn, causes of homelessness were perceived as structural (low wages, exploitation, a lack of jobs, bad schools), while welfare dependency was perceived as resulting from individual/personal causes (lifestyle choices, abilities and talents, morals and drunkenness, lack of effort). Two participants in this study, Jude and Vincent, resisted the idea that a majority of St. Louis's unhoused population was Black, which contradicts both my experience as an ethnographer and statistics from the annual point-in-time count conducted by the U.S. Department of Housing and Urban Development (2017b,a). The fact that homelessness is a popular public and academic concern (B. A. Lee, Tyler, and Wright 2010) may be related to the perception of homelessness as a white issue. How do racial politics and the racialization of homelessness affect services on an interactional level as white and/or middle-class volunteers come into contact with St. Louis's predominantly Black homeless population?

(Poverty) Tourism

Tourism is a social and spatial phenomenon in which tourists are attracted to a place by the promise of exploration in an unfamiliar place or of an Other (Bauman 1998; Minca 2000). With cultural experiences continuing to grow as an object for consumption, spatial contexts have transformed to meet the needs/demands of consumers. Resorts, theme parks, and tourist towns have emerged as "protected and closed spaces which offer the over-abundance of image stimuli to which we have become accustomed" (Minca 2000, 401). Other tourist attractions seek to provide experiences of "authenticity," meaning that they are perceived as genuine products of local culture(s) and/or deemed traditional in some way, shape, or form (Chhabra, Healy, and Sills 2003; Urry 1990). Such spaces are evaluated by a tourist gaze that "presupposes a system of social activities and signs which locate the particular tourist practices, not in terms of some intrinsic characteristics, but through the contrasts implied with non-tourist social practices, particularly those based within the home and paid work" (Urry 1990, 2). Thus, authenticity is measured by a space's or a people's ability to meet expectations (or stereotypes) of social or cultural difference.

Around the world and especially in the Global South, tourists increasingly seek this perceived authenticity in slums, and a growing body of literature seeks to understand the slum, poverty, and volunteer tourism industries (Frenzel et al. 2015; Roy 2011). These industries trade on the idea of consumable culturally authentic experiences (Crossley 2012; Dyson 2012; Frenzel 2016; Frisch 2012; Kontogeorgopoulos 2016; Lasker 2016; A. J. McIntosh and Zahra 2007; Schneider 2018) and the ability to mix social responsibility with observation of poverty, adventure, and entertainment—tours, bars, restaurants, concerts, festivals, and even bungee jumping (Butler 2012; Frenzel 2016). Many poverty tours advertise themselves as "reality tours" to emphasize the "authentic" experiences tourists will gain—experiences that may or may not conceptualize poverty as the defining feature of the slum (Meschkank 2011).

Much debate exists around practices of poverty tourism (Freire-Medeiros 2013). Some observers argue that poverty and volunteer tourism can be a tool for development/modernization, empowerment of the poor, and poverty alleviation (Frenzel 2013, 2016; D. Harrison 2008; Scheyvens 2001); cultural exchange (A. J. McIntosh and Zahra 2007; Scheyvens 2001); or social justice (Conran 2011; Scheyvens 2001). Proponents of this view draw attention to the tourist industry's ability to bring income to previously avoided communities and residents (D. Harrison 2008; Scheyvens 2001). In addition, Regina Scheyvens (2001) contends that ethical standards of poverty tourism are a crucial part of its definition and that any form of voyeurism or pity-motivated volunteering would be at odds with poverty tourism. Instead, poverty/slum tours are well served by emphasizing "true" life and everyday cultural practices in the toured area, in effect undermining conceptions of the slum as places of suffering, hardship, and despair (Meschkank 2011).

This picture of poverty tourism constitutes a system of best practices rather than as a definition grounded in a regularly observed reality. A number of scholars have argued that in practice, poverty tourism is voyeuristic and Otherizing (Dovey and King 2012; Dürr and Jaffe 2012) and brings legacies of colonialism into the neoliberal era (Manyara and Jones 2007). Poverty tourism may Otherize those living in slums because the experience does not constitute an opportunity to build cross-cultural connections; instead, tourists and volunteers observe poverty as an object of difference (Crossley 2012; Simpson 2004). Although tourists frequently express an interest in learning from the host community, conceptions of poverty, culture, and race are also deployed as a means of maintaining social and physical distance (Crossley 2012; Schneider 2018; Simpson 2004). Despite the stated goals of community development and cultural exchange, many slum tours are operated by people who are not members of the subject community, and many fail to initiate interaction between community members and tourists (Frisch 2012).

Although attention to common pitfalls might permit poverty tourism to offer opportunities for poverty alleviation and for cultural understanding (Scheyvens 2007), proponents of poverty tourism must still grapple with the tourist gaze (Frisch 2012). The slum is theorized as an ideal tourist location because it offers a largely privileged group of people a chance to observe a world believed to be the opposite of their own (Freire-Medeiros 2013). On the one hand, the tourist's desire to gaze on the slum opens up opportunities for transformation (Dovey and King 2012). On the other hand, tourists seek "authentic" experiences based on preconceived notions of the Other. As tourists flock to these locations, images of the slum as a place of squalor and despair or as a place where people are poor but happy are reproduced and disseminated through selective photography and tourist narratives (Crossley 2012; Dürr and Jaffe 2012). Given that tourists are drawn to an aestheticized poverty (Dovey and King 2012; Dürr and Jaffe 2012), poverty tourism might have difficulty providing sustainable improvements to the community and alleviating poverty on a large scale without compromising the slum's appeal to tourists.

Poverty tourism is typically though not exclusively associated with the Global South (Freire-Medeiros 2013; Frenzel 2015; Steinbrink 2012). Fabian Frenzel and colleagues (2015) estimate that more than one million people go on slum tours each year, with more than 80 percent of these tours taking place in the favelas of

Brazil or the townships of South Africa. The homeless service activities I observed were neither formally planned slum tours nor exotic excursions to foreign lands where the people were perceived to be poor in market opportunities but rich in culture (Crossley 2012; Kontogeorgopoulos 2016). Nevertheless, many volunteers displayed a touristic impulse. In St. Louis, observed volunteers, both Black and white, both color-blind and color-conscious, repeatedly professed interest in "urban decay" and took photos with such frequency that one volunteer jokingly asked if another volunteer "ever feels like a Japanese tourist." In these moments, volunteers sought to explore their home city in a way that few others of their class status would, in the process emphasizing the difference between themselves and those on the street.

The Draw of the "Derelicts"

Many of the volunteers conceptualized their efforts in touristic terms. They desired to observe an "elsewhere" (Bauman 1998). With most participants coming from middle-class households and many of them coming from suburban areas, homeless outreach doubled as an adventure into marginal, physically crumbling, graffiti-riddled urban space, a chance to tour the peculiar lives of those excluded from "normal" life (Freire-Medeiros 2013; Urry 1990). As Teresa, a white woman who was among the most consistent volunteers with Right Choice Ministry and Outreach, explained,

> When I was younger, I was always interested in the "derelicts," shall we say. I was always interested in that which was not normal. I was always kind of curious, but I was always told, "Don't go there. Don't do this. If you go through a bad area, just drop your head, don't be seen." But I was always kind of curious as to what was going on, and it kind of grew more into that role when I got older.

She then decided to act on that curiosity through Right Choice service opportunities, seeking more information about people living outside "normal" white middle-class life.

Another white Right Choice volunteer, Veronica, explained that when she learned about the group at her church's involvement fair, she was "intrigued." She began attending outreach events and came to enjoy service activities as a chance to learn:

> At first . . . I was nervous. I didn't know how to react or what to say to people. But once you get to know our homeless friends, they're just like me and you, just different circumstances on how they're living, and [you can] talk to them like you

would talk to anybody. . . . Just the way that they can live and survive, I guess, in a different climate was interesting to me—how some want to stay in that lifestyle, some don't. I just like hearing their stories and getting to know the people.

People experiencing homelessness thus constituted an attraction of sorts. Even if what the volunteers learned was not wholly accurate (e.g., that people choose to be homeless), performing homeless outreach was enjoyable because it gave them an opportunity to witness life on the margins. By going out on a regular basis to serve their "friends," people "just like me and you," volunteers also had the opportunity to witness something fascinating: how someone could "survive" in a "different climate." This sense of Otherness was embedded in the desire to volunteer, to observe this phenomenon firsthand. Whether that difference was real or imagined mattered little to volunteers, who were just as likely to perceive people experiencing homelessness as like the volunteers themselves as to emphasize the opposite.

Emphasizing Otherness

On December 14, 2017, members of Fellowship Outreach set out on their normal Thursday night route. After making several stops across St. Louis, including two in downtown and one on the east side of the Mississippi River, we pulled up to our final stop, on the west bank. We could see barges floating down the river; in the distance, the bridges between Missouri and Illinois were visible despite the darkness. We were there to visit with "friends" Clark and Lynn. Peter walked along the floodwall to their tent hidden among the trees and brush to fetch them for conversation and supplies. He returned without them, however, and reported that for the second week in a row, their camp was there but they were not.

Perhaps a bit disappointed, the members of the group started to retreat to their cars. Peter, however, approached a black tarp a few paces from where the group had been standing that had escaped everyone else's notice. The tarp turned out to be covering a parked car, and Peter called out to ask whether anyone was there and whether they needed food or supplies. Someone emerged: Lance, a young Black man wearing a Southeast Missouri State University hoodie. We were used to seeing Lance at a South Side gathering spot, and Peter greeted him warmly. Lance was given chips, donuts, and chicken sandwiches, and as he awkwardly crawled under the tarp to tuck the supplies into the car, Peter chuckled, "This is a first," and took a series of photos. Peter and likely others present perceived Lance's poverty as a spectacle, contrasting not only with everyday suburban or middle-class life but also with other encounters with people experiencing homelessness. We stayed only long enough to learn that Lance had a friend somewhere nearby and that he had not seen Clark or Lynn. Throughout this exchange and as we retreated to our cars, Peter continued to take photos of Lance's tarp-covered car.

The concept of tourism is built on the perceived contrast between leisure and work, between one's "real" life and one's experiences "elsewhere" (Minca 2000; Urry 1990). Likewise, homeless outreach appealed to volunteers at least in part because it provided them with an opportunity to observe alternative practices of living as novelty. Because such a series of events would not be commonplace in the more affluent suburban neighborhoods in which the volunteers resided, the chance to observe a man crawling in and out of a tarp-covered car was an attraction. The group stood circled around, chuckling while Peter took photos, explicitly noting the novelty of the experience by saying, "This is a first." Creating such spectacle out of homeless life was a regular occurrence, though Peter and the others did not necessarily do so with any malice. Although Peter is a remarkably genuine and well-intentioned person, his comments and actions were seemingly driven by a touristic impulse that reenforced the difference between his social position and that of Lance. By taking photos, making social media posts, and strolling through dwellings without consent, volunteers who were there to "help" reified the difference between those living in homelessness or poverty and those living in financially secure households.

Homelessness and the Volunteer Gaze

After volunteer groups identified and traveled to appropriate space(s), their statuses and mission as volunteers enabled them to begin exploring both places and people. Although mildly tense moments occurred on rare occasions, interactions between volunteers and people experiencing homelessness were almost always friendly, and many volunteers reported enjoying outreach. But volunteers' enjoyment of such forms of service provision did not result solely from the friendly nature of these interactions, a feeling of being appreciated, or the development of relationships; rather, the enjoyment also resulted from the ability to observe the marginal and to learn about the Other. Volunteers' outreach brought them into contact with another St. Louis that they would or could not experience during the "normal" course of their lives. They sought a firsthand knowledge of homeless difference that could be obtained only through "authentic" experiences. Claire's interactions, for example, resulted in what she described as "magic moments":

> Maybe a year or two ago, and we were going different places. A lot of the homeless people will have jobs. I mean, it's literally they don't have enough to make ends meet. They are working. They don't have enough money for a place. It's

crazy. So this guy he had a bike. He had a job interview. He was so sweet. And he ended up singing for us. He had this incredible voice, soulful voice. And then we sang with him, and stuff like that. You can't pay for that. And [there was] the guy with the typewriter that was writing poems for everybody. How do you get experiences like that? The only way you can is if you do stuff like this. This is stuff I will remember forever.

Claire understood her experiences as sharply contrasting with her daily life in a rural town as well as with other generic forms of leisure. Rather than having the cookie-cutter experiences for which tourists might pay, she voyaged into places unknown filled with people unknown and was often rewarded with unique experiences.

Claire found her experience with the typewriter poet significant enough that she posted about it on a public social media site: "I was given a typewritten poem by a young homeless guy (who also happened to be brilliantly creative); I will keep it forever. I promised I would write him a poem in return. I hope you can enjoy it too!" She did not share the man's poem but posted the one she wrote for him:

FIGURE 8. An unhoused man plays his guitar for a volunteer, while another volunteer talks to an unhoused man sitting on the step of an abandoned building, June 3, 2021. © Matthew Jerome Schneider.

Street-Alex[2] wrote me a poem.
I asked him to.
Joyfully he ripped out bright yellow backing
From a notebook;
Stuck it in an ancient typewriter,
Listened and spoke as he wrote:
His third poem in a row.
I thought, perhaps, I would end up with the leavings,
The tired remains from his first two works.
I'm so excited to do this,
He was saying . . .
I have this gift, I can see into a soul
Write what the person is feeling, going through,
Needs.
Cynicism is the catchword of the day.
Yet his first poem,
About love-light-giving—
What we were feebly attempting to do—
Was really magnificent.
So then he read mine.
I expected, if his gift was real,
To hear of pain, struggle—
Grief.
Instead, he wrote of choices:
To choose to live, to love, to be free
Despite constraints.
Not what I expected; but true; very true;
And soft tears came to my eyes:
A soul-response, a heart answer
Apart from mind, thought, memory.
His namesake, I think, is Alyosha—Alexei—
From *Brothers Karamozov* [*sic*]:
A mystic, a poet;
A giver as well.
I told him I would write a poem for him in return.
How to do it while avoiding
Condescension, false intimacy,
Over-romanticism?
To Alex:
I have now
A torn piece of paper
With typewritten words
And a memory—a spot of time—
Of a soul which chooses to give,

Which finds joy in helping others
In a form most unique.
I will keep this gift, Alex,
And the memory of the beautiful typewriter
And the street
And the cold
And unafraid, unassuming boldness:
The confidence of freedom,
In a city-street in the dark, in the night
Full of light.

Her post not only highlighted the perceived intimacy of her fleeting connection to "Street-Alex" but signaled her intent for another audience to derive meaning from it. She wanted readers to know about the lasting impact the experience has had on her and used her poem as evidence of her expedition to find something/someone interesting. In addition, she presented an argument for her view of homelessness: in spite of his cold, hard life, this man remained brilliant, creative, generous, and "full of light." She took it upon herself to convince the world that although Alex existed on the margins, he had value. Nevertheless, the narrative she (re)produced was one of "choices," "unassuming boldness," and "confidence of freedom," regardless of "constraints."

FIGURE 9. A vacated encampment on the East Side not far from Enos's camp, May 29, 2021. © Matthew Jerome Schneider.

Experiences between volunteers and Alex and people like him played an important role in the crafting of volunteer narratives about homelessness. The perceived intimacy of these unique moments or of volunteers' relationships with specific people experiencing homelessness could be leveraged to reproduce a particular view of homelessness that emphasized individual morality over structural oppression (Conran 2011). Thus, even as Claire advanced an understanding of individual people experiencing homelessness as bold, resilient, and talented, she reduced Alex to a character whose creative gifts were most notable because she encountered him on her adventures in St. Louis's urban backstage.

Claire's decision to post her reflections in this particular online space seems to have been unusual, though the taking of photos was not and served a similar purpose.[3] On the evening of April 9, 2018, while I was conversing around a barrel fire with two other volunteers, John moved around the fire, snapping photos of us with his phone. He then started to post those photos on a social media site and interrupted the group conversation to ask whether I wanted to be tagged in the post because he does not tag people without their permission. (On a previous occasion, however, he had tagged me in a post without my consent, and he did not ask the men being served for permission to post their photos.) The other volunteers and I did not object to being tagged, and the resulting post included a number of photos of people gathered around the smoky fire as well as a close-up selfie of John and Scott, a Black man experiencing homelessness whose smile prominently featured a missing tooth. John subsequently took more photos, asking David, another Black man experiencing homelessness, to pose with a group of volunteers and capturing images of Dominic, an older white volunteer, and Scott hugging and "goofing around," as John put it.

Like Claire, John sought to document his experience in marginal space in a way that gave him a claim to authenticity, to an observed reality. He and other members of Right Choice and Fellowship nearly always took photos of people experiencing homelessness and spaces (thought to be) occupied by the unhoused. Smoky bonfires, graffiti-covered walls, tents, crumbling redbrick buildings, and abandoned warehouses were treated as tourist destinations. Such images highlighted the perceived destitution of St. Louis's fringe urban landscape or perhaps the ingenuity and resilience of life on the margins, while the selfies and "goofing around" photos demonstrated to social media followers that John and Right Choice had cultivated genuine connections with the homeless Other.[4]

Both Claire and John cast their tourist gaze on homeless subjects. That gaze is built on two interlocking conditions. First, tourists must perceive the experience as in some way authentic or genuine. This perception largely rests on their ability to frame the experience as both different from "normal" life and as in alignment with preconceived notions of what the experience should be like. This work, of course, is often informed by the consumption of media (e.g., social media photos, movies) that have taught tourists what differences they should expect to encounter (Urry 1990). Kim Dovey and Ross King (2012, 287) suggest that poverty tourism is appealing because it offers the chance to observe an "informal" and "impenetrable" urban "labyrinth." Volunteering thus offers a chance to glimpse a "backstage" St. Louis that is otherwise off-limits to those coming from the formal city (Kontogeorgopoulos 2016; MacCannell 1973, 1992).

Second, the tourist gaze relies on visual stimulation. Above all else, tourist interactions are framed by the difference in visual surroundings (Urry 1990, 1992). The physical surroundings provided a stunning backdrop for the homelessness observed by volunteers, as John's photos of the landscape demonstrated.

With these two conditions met, tourists often reproduce understandings of the slum. Photographs and other documentation of encounters are significant in this process. As John Urry (1990, 139) contends, photographs suggest knowledge of and power over the captured object. And although photographs are generally interpreted as transcriptions of reality, they "are the outcome of a signifying practice in which those taking the photo select, structure and shape what is go-

FIGURE 10. A graffiti-covered building that regularly serves as shelter for people experiencing homelessness and that prompts some volunteers to take photographs. © Matthew Jerome Schneider.

ing to be taken" (139; see also Sekula 1982). Thus, as John, Claire, and other volunteers document their experiences with people experiencing homelessness, they (re)construct meanings of homelessness, poverty, and life deemed not normal. This constructed meaning of "authentic" homelessness—which is largely accepted as real but is implicitly framed by preconceived understandings about homeless difference—then becomes further entrenched as this documentation is shared with other volunteers, friends, congregation members, and online followers (Dürr and Jaffe 2012; Sekula 1981, 1982; Urry 1990, 1992). These photographs, reflections, and intragroup conversations certainly reflect a reality, but this reality is filtered through classed and racialized perceptions.

The motivations for slum tourism and homeless outreach volunteering are remarkably similar, but the tourist gaze might also be applied to all volunteers who seek face-to-face interaction with people in disadvantaged positions, including but not limited to programs such as Teach for America and the Peace Corps and white antiracist activist organizations. E. Gil Clary and Mark Snyder (1999) have developed a typology of six social-psychological volunteer motivations: values-based (volunteer feels it is important to help others), a desire to better understand the world or to develop otherwise unused skills, a belief that volunteering will lead to some sort of personal growth, a desire to obtain career-related experience or skills, a belief that volunteering will allow the volunteer to strengthen or create social relationships, and a desire to reduce a person's negative feelings (guilt). The volunteers with whom I interacted expressed all of these motivations to some degree, but the motivation to understand or learn about homelessness stood out. The volunteer tourism literature has established that volunteers are often motivated by the idea of experiencing something new, exotic, and/or "authentic" (Kontogeorgopoulos 2016; A. J. McIntosh and Zahra 2007; Schneider 2018; Tiessen 2012). This gaze need not be limited to geographic boundaries or activities that more closely resemble traditional tourism. With nearly all volunteers coming from some position of privilege (class, racial, and/or residential), homeless service represents an opportunity to explore an "elsewhere" (Bauman 1998) as volunteers undertake a quest for understanding. This gaze is racialized based on volunteers' racial ideologies, and their understandings of race and social inequality more generally shaped the way they interacted with the space, their conclusions about homelessness (which they confirmed rather than developed), and the information they disseminated to others through photos, conversation, and social media.

A Racialized Volunteer Gaze

Like many other social processes, the volunteer gaze was racialized in the context of homeless service provision. Variance in racial ideology across the groups produced at least two forms of volunteer gaze. Many volunteers, principally those coming from Citywide Outreach, Fam in the Streets, Mercy House, and Service House, operated based on color-conscious social- and racial-justice-oriented ideologies. Members of these groups openly grappled with systemic racism and thought of poverty and racial inequality in structural terms. Many belonged to other explicitly antiracist organizations and expressed interest in working for systemic change, most frequently at the level of city government. Conversely, they were also likely to express an interest in consuming Black culture, which in some instances was conflated with homelessness/poverty (Harris 2001; Kirschenman and Neckerman 1991). This desire was perhaps most pronounced among white volunteers at Mercy House, many of whom lived or had lived in the North Side shelter as a part of their dedication to (or a perk of) the mission.

On one November 2017 morning, I volunteered alongside Paul, handing out sandwiches and donated clothes. Very few people came by, and we were passing the time in the Mercy House office. While Paul worked on the volunteer schedule, I flipped through a book I found on the desk, Shelly Tochluk's *Witnessing Whiteness* (2010), written for a white antiracist audience. I noticed that Paul had flagged a paragraph by writing "me :(" in the margin

> For me, part of my journey involved a wholesale rejection of my home community, my culture, and my sense of self. I fell into a troubling pattern that many distressed whites demonstrate. Part of that included unwittingly objectifying people of color as I turned to them in escape of my "white" life. I retreated into a world of color, what many describe as "colorful" garb, "colorful" music, and "colorful" people. At that time, I had much antipathy for anything that reminded me of my former, less aware, white self. I found conversations with most white people on matters of race fruitless. I now see that those conversations failed, in part, because they were not in the spirit of two people sharing dialogue. They were arguments, meant to bolster my view of the world and break theirs down. (vii)

I asked Paul to elaborate on the frown they had drawn, and they explained that they had joined Mercy House's core community as a consequence of feelings similar to Tochluk's:

> I've always been interested in other cultures or other people that aren't just like me. But I remember a very very vivid—I'm surprised it came this early—moment when I had just failed all my finals in my second year of [college], and I was read-

ing the *People's History of the United States* (Zinn 1980) because I was feeling incredibly anxious and didn't want to go to sleep, and just like freaking out. . . . It's awesome. I only got like a third of the way through it. It's just talking about the history of the United States from oppressed peoples' perspective. And I was realizing how fucked up everything was and how this country was founded on genocide and slavery and thinking about how I care about these things in the front of my brain, but at the end of the day, I like my little white privilege bubble. I explore those spaces and talk about those things, but I like privilege and I like my position of power in this society. I just remember having this image of this little cocoon that I nestle back into, which is comforting myself with all my privileges. I think that my life since then has been about trying to dig deeper, figure out what's going on there. Because I knew that was wrong when I felt that. I was never satisfied with—I mean, I was for a long time, but I didn't feel satisfied in that moment in paying lip service to the fight for justice and then just going back to my normal life.

Seeking to contribute to social and racial justice, Paul moved into a predominantly Black neighborhood to live and work at a shelter for women, children, and trans people experiencing homelessness.

Other volunteers were drawn to volunteer work in poor Black neighborhoods because they wanted to contest racist assumptions about those neighborhoods and their residents. Ambrose, a Mercy House volunteer, explained that he wanted to challenge "the beliefs that I was taught," while Tatiana, a Citywide Outreach volunteer, sought a "sense of breaking down the us and them." But while racial justice-minded volunteers were moved to service and activism after recognizing that racial inequality did not align with their morals (Warren 2010), their efforts were also tied to interest in unfamiliar cultures and people. That is, they sought to escape white spaces. Paul differentiated themself from other color-conscious volunteers through the ability to be reflexive.

Nevertheless, Paul and other volunteers who had relatively strong understandings of historical and structural oppression of minority groups often failed to fully recognize the power of their privileged positions. Black urban space was essentialized not only as poor and disadvantaged (Hughey 2007; Hunter and Robinson 2016; W. J. Wilson 1987) but also as offering an escape from the "white privilege bubble" where volunteers could relate to the oppressed on an "authentic" and interpersonal level (Hughey 2007). While driven by the desire to work for social and/or racial justice, these volunteers utilized a canned set of racial stereotypes to decide where to direct their gaze.

Many other volunteers, mostly from Fellowship and Right Choice, operated through individualistic color-blind ideologies. These volunteers minimized the importance of race in the reproduction of homelessness and social inequality and were especially dismissive of the idea that race informed their service activities. However, these volunteers typically cast their gaze on predominantly white homeless spaces. Perhaps because homelessness is perceived as a white issue (G. Wilson 1996), color-blind volunteers spent time consuming these spaces as "authentic" representations of homeless life. But they could not totally ignore the overrepresentation of Black people in the unhoused population. While one color-blind volunteer, Claire, conceded that "sadly, it seems like white volunteers tend to get along the best with white homeless people," color-blind volunteers more commonly deflected questions about the disproportionate amount of time they spent socializing in predominantly white camps.

On the evening of June 10, 2018, I rode with John of Right Choice Ministry and Outreach. After parting with "our homeless friends" on the North Side, we stopped to check in on Stan. As we pulled up to the abandoned warehouse in which he lived, we saw a fairly large gathering of African American men and women who seemed to be experiencing homelessness. They were camped out in the shade of a few trees across the narrow blacktop from the warehouse; bags and trash were strewn about, and a couple of the people were sitting in folding chairs. When I asked John what was going on, he responded, "Oh, they've been there. A bunch of trouble is what this is."

Right Choice volunteers commonly bypassed groups of mostly Black men on the streets between downtown and the North Side. Because Fam in the Streets usually stopped at these locations, I knew not only that many of these people were experiencing homelessness but also that they were friendly and welcoming. Based on the places where these people gathered (near the city shelter and abandoned buildings) and their appearance (unwashed or ill-fitting clothes), the volunteers should have realized that these people would have been receptive to a stop by an outreach group. Yet night after night, the Right Choice caravan ignored them in favor of providing food, supplies, and conversation to a group of mostly white men living in a comparatively well-stocked camp in Illinois on the east side of the river. On this particular night, John articulated why these groups were to be avoided, but he did so by relying on a shared understanding of the context and of the racially coded word "trouble" (Burke 2012). In so doing, he avoided breaking the rules of color-blind discourse.

On another occasion, John explained that he was uncomfortable stopping for gas in certain parts of the city because drug deals might be going on at the gas stations. Justin, who had lived on the predominantly Black North Side during a year of service, told us confidently that a sound "wasn't a knock at the door" but a gunshot. Ana continued to volunteer despite objections from family members who feared for her safety. Other Fellowship Outreach volunteers insisted that if danger arose, they would receive protection from their "homeless friends." In a presentation to nonvolunteers, Simon, a white Citywide volunteer, called attention to perceived danger by reflecting on a night when he asked himself, "How did I end up driving this van around in the dark in North City?" While his mostly older and white listeners laughed at the idea, Simon added, "But I felt confident doing it," highlighting a potential gap between perception and reality.[5]

As a white man always accompanied by at least one other volunteer, I never felt myself to be threatened or in danger during the many hours I spent on the North Side and transporting Black men to shelter. While feelings of safety are subjective, commonly racialized beliefs about particular types of people and urban spaces governed volunteer decisions and actions. For groups with a bent toward color blindness, the interactions and locations they were willing to serve were informed by race. Fellowship was less selective than Right Choice about whom to serve, but the differences I witnessed in volunteers' approaches based on service location were striking. When we stopped at gathering places in or near downtown that primarily attracted Black men, the caravan of vehicles would pull up and the volunteers would make their way to the car carrying the supplies. Then they would ask the people experiencing homelessness about what food and other provisions were needed and distribute those items. For several minutes thereafter, most volunteers would talk among themselves while the people served would retreat to their previous locations, although a handful of conversations between volunteers and service recipients might also take place. From time to time, a volunteer would venture into the space where people experiencing homelessness loitered or slept to see what was going on or to offer supplies to someone who had not approached the caravan, but the social atmosphere varied considerably from that observed in predominantly white gathering places.

In predominantly white locations, including a number of smaller camps, the social atmosphere was almost always lively. Volunteers and service recipients traded stories about their lives and talked about local and national politics, jobs, mutual acquaintances, and local events. According to Fellowship's Bernard, one of his daughter's

> favorite stops and probably my favorite stops too is going over to Enos's [all-white] camp. Hot chocolate and a campfire—that's not a half bad time, you know. But my least favorite stop is going to—well, it's not there anymore, we stopped, but when we were going to that park, that last stop. That's my least favorite stop because that is where the interactions have been the worst. Even [at a church near

downtown], those were always pretty good. Most of those [Black] guys, you talk to them, and they're thankful for bringing you "what you got." That park, that element over there, which is predominantly younger—not all, but predominantly younger—there's always a harsher reaction with those folks over there.

Bernard criticized nearly all people experiencing homelessness, characterizing it as a choice to be unproductive, but he preferred the time spent with the predominantly white group at Enos's camp on the east side of the river. Despite Bernard's claims that his preferences related to age and/or willingness to show gratitude, his reference to "what you got" was a callback to an earlier portion of the interview and an imitation of American Black English. He previously stated that

> A lot of them are—they'll take what you're giving them, but they're not very thankful. They're not particularly nice. Some of them are. Don't get me wrong. It's not all of them. But a lot of them, especially the younger ones. The older guys are much more gentlemen: "Thank you, sir. God bless you, thank you." That kind of thing. But the younger guys, guys who are in their 20s and 30s won't, maybe, not say shit to you: "What you got?" They act like thugs, you know.[6]

Bernard tied his less negative assessment of the predominantly Black group at the church to members' willingness to express gratitude for the group's help—that is, to acknowledge contributions from and be appropriately deferential to people with superior social status.

Bernard exemplified a racialized (or racist) volunteer gaze. Although he saw some value in serving those experiencing homelessness, the process of identifying consumable spaces was based on racist stereotypes and preconceptions. At the all-white camp on the east side of the river, Bernard could relax and have a good time. But when he ventured into spaces occupied by predominantly Black groups, his expectations changed. Rather than seeing these moments as opportunities to have hot chocolate and conversation with "homeless friends," he expected Black men experiencing homelessness to take handouts and express gratitude. Variation from this pattern signaled either ingratitude, as in Bernard's case, or danger, as in John's.

Touring Homelessness?

The volunteers in this study form part of a larger pattern of well-intentioned people from privileged positions pursuing the dual but contradictory goals of learning about or exploring the Other and contributing to their neighbors' well-being. While activities that more closely resemble traditional tourism (e.g., volunteer tourism, slum tourism) have been questioned and their merits debated (A. J. McIntosh and Zahra 2007; Raymond and Hall 2008; Simpson 2004), more attention should be given to volunteer and activist efforts to address social inequalities.

In this study, volunteers expressed a desire not only to serve but to learn about homelessness through firsthand experiences (Clary and Snyder 1999). As with slum tourism, this learning process involved exploring beyond the social and physical boundaries of the formal city in search of an authentic homelessness to observe (Dovey and King 2012; Kontogeorgopoulos 2016; MacCannell 1973, 1992). This process was often based on and helped reproduce preconceived ideas about the meanings of homelessness. These volunteers cast a touristic gaze on people and settings that could affirm preexisting (or slightly modified) views of homelessness (Urry 1990, 1992). The volunteers' gaze was intertwined with their racial ideologies. Those who entered service with color-conscious views of social inequality plunged themselves into settings where they could consume an idealized and "authentic" Black poverty. Color-blind volunteers, conversely, conceptualized white homelessness as difference but Black homelessness as danger, a product of laziness, and/or a symptom of cultural deficiency. These differing gazes translated into differing volunteer practices. For example, relying on a gaze that constructs Black homelessness as danger likely results in the uneven distribution of resources, with greater amounts of time and a greater share of resources going to groups that are predominantly white or are well-known to the volunteer group members.

The volunteer gaze draws volunteers—a largely white, college-educated, middle-class group of people (Foster-Bey 2008)—toward what Teresa described as "the derelicts." This gaze also reproduces and reifies existing social relationships among volunteers, volunteers and service recipients, and mainstream society and homeless Others. These volunteers offered tangible benefits to St. Louis's homeless population, providing shelter, transportation, blankets, propane, food, and other items that literally saved lives. Furthermore, as Mark R. Warren (2010) explains, witnessing (racial) inequality is an important first step toward activist mobilization. However, volunteer organizations serving marginalized groups must grapple with the volunteer gaze in the same way that slum tourist organizations must interrogate the tourist gaze—that is, to prevent the reproduction of the Otherizing narratives on which the gazes rely.

CONCLUSION

"I Want White People to Be Better"

Excerpt of an Interview with Catherine
Lower-Middle-Class White Volunteer with
Mercy House
December 1, 2017

Catherine: I feel like [Mercy House] was always attempting to go against the grain, and that's why I stayed for that long. That's why I stayed for four years, and that's why I still mess with them—because I think it's different. It's always evolving and getting better. . . . Me being critical of it isn't necessarily totally dismissing it or whatever. I just always want it to be better. You know what I mean—I want white people to be better. I want white people to undo their whiteness. I want white people to get rid of that culture, because if we got rid of that, we wouldn't even have as big of fucking problems as we do, systematically in our communities and in ourselves. I think that it's important to have that tough love. It's important to not throw away people. It's important not to throw away things, in a sense of—I don't hate Mercy House. I don't say "Fuck this or that." But I really loved it. I want it to get better, so I'm not going to just live in—what do you call it—rose-colored glasses or whatever. I'm not going to sit around and say that it's great all the time, because it wasn't.

Toward Reflexive Antiracist Service and Activism

Marginalized communities and populations can mobilize around any number of social and civic problems to create change for themselves. However, such action can be time consuming and expensive, can require considerable social and political capital, and/or can require volunteers/activists to overcome structural obstacles (Cloward and Piven 1984; Cress and Snow 1996; B. A. Lee, Tyler, and Wright 2010). Thus, it is both ironic and unsurprising that so much of the work needed to provide for the "most vulnerable among us" is carried out by people in privileged social positions, often through religious and activist organizations (Foster-Bey 2008; Musick and Wilson 2008; Pho 2008; Wasserman and Clair 2010; J. Wilson 2012).

This volume is broadly situated in the fields of racial and ethnic relations, social inequalities, urban sociology, civic engagement, and tourism. With an emphasis on race, class, and privileged housing/neighborhood status, this book has explored the relationship between community service and privilege as well as how service interactions may reproduce, undermine, or shape systems of inequality in spite of volunteers' intentions to the contrary. What motivates people of privileged positions to seek out interpersonal experiences with people living on the margins? How do race, class, and/or ideology inform the interactions between these groups? How do these interactions undermine or (re)produce the structural constraints facing the service population?

Volunteer outreach, local response, and nonprofit work is all the more important because state and federal support for people in extreme poverty has long proven inadequate (Edin and Shaefer 2015; Hackworth 2012; Lyon-Callo 2015; Rogers 2017; Willse 2015). At the same time, volunteerism as it is currently conceptualized and practiced by people of privileged positions faces its own challenges. Although many volunteers are incredibly inspiring, dedicated, and kind-hearted people, they are subject to structural disciplining, and the practices in which many of these people regularly engage must be critically interrogated.

Chapter 1 explored how meaning was derived, modified, and entrenched through interaction within volunteer groups. After finding a group that presented palatable ideas about poverty, race, urban space, and service values, volunteers would frequently turn to each other to shore up their views on homelessness and group purpose. Rather than root or amend their understandings of homelessness based on interactions with service recipients, group members relied on repeated conversations with people in similar positions. In particular, volunteers commonly reproduced narratives about sin (e.g., laziness, exploiting volunteer generosity, dishonesty), systems (e.g., failures of the city government, institutional racism), and sickness (e.g., mental illness, addiction).

Chapter 2 focused on two groups that endeavored to provide charity on the streets. Both organizations relied heavily on individualized understandings of homelessness and a color-blind view of the world. Specifically, they pointed to common stereotypes about homelessness—as a choice, the consequence of laziness, or as the result of addiction or poor mental health—to justify this approach to service. In so doing, group members simultaneously dismissed race as unimportant and dedicated more time, resources, and emotional labor to white people experiencing homelessness.

Chapter 3 highlighted the experiences of explicitly color-conscious volunteers. As a race scholar and advocate for racial justice, I see the task of cultivating a color-conscious, antiracist society as absolutely necessary. However, these volunteers demonstrate the current limits of white allyship. So although 57 percent of Americans, including 47 percent of white Americans, agree that "white people benefit at least a fair amount from advantages that Black people do not have" (Pew 2021), understanding race as group position needs additional emphasis. Even white volunteers who were willing to consider the structural dimensions of inequality and racism generally failed to situate their experiences within broader social patterns that they help reproduce—that is, most could not conceptualize whiteness as a group position of privilege affecting everyday interactions. Because their whiteness did not create structural obstacles for them to overcome, many understood their race as an inconsequential personal trait that could be managed. Volunteers—particularly white volunteers providing services to nonwhite populations—must understand that race, volunteer status, and class status represent a set of power relations that cannot be disentangled from (inter)actions. Racial categories and boundaries are, after all, the result of long-standing conflict, with the white racial category reproducing its dominance through institutionalization of its power and disproportionate access to social, political, and economic resources (Blumer 1958; Doane 1997; Lipsitz 1998; Omi and Winant 1994; Wellman 1993).

Finally, chapter 4 theorized the existence of a volunteer gaze. Given their privileged positions and particularly their residence in suburban neighborhoods, volunteers defined homelessness by its difference. The desire to explore this difference was a driving force behind (sustained) volunteering. Although the volunteer gaze may have been useful in mobilizing people for service provision, it might also problematically resemble the practice of slum/poverty tourism. As volunteers sought out "authentic" homeless Others and explored the informal city, they emphasized the marginality of those they served and the spaces they navigated. Cultural meanings attached to notions of homelessness varied based on the group's ideological bent. The gaze of groups that approached service with a color-blind ideology reproduced white homelessness simply as difference. These volunteers generally sympathized with whites experiencing homelessness despite raising questions about work ethic and motivation. Black homelessness, conversely, was often associated with danger and ingratitude/undeservingness. By contrast, color-conscious organizations emphasized Blackness as a cultural product ripe for consumption. Seeking such experiences, members of these groups engaged in a racial project that (re)constructed Blackness as a culturally rich yet static position of poverty and oppression.

This book presents a complicated picture of volunteering. Goodwill and positive intentions alone are not enough in the face of structural problems such as homelessness and racial inequality. Nevertheless, these volunteers have recognized a real problem in their community and sought to do something about it, which is particularly noteworthy in light of the municipal government's failure to do so. The question, then, is how these volunteers and groups can engage with their communities in a way that will work more effectively toward the stated goals.

Responding to Structural Limitations

Volunteers across groups frequently lamented their inability to "change situations" and/or spur systemic change. Fellowship Outreach's Peter felt that he was limited to

> pointing [people experiencing homelessness] to different agencies that help with certain things or sharing my own story, which was a gift to me—to hear from other addicts that have gotten clean, that's a strength to us. . . . You get the folks that could be housed if they get to Florida or Los Angeles or New Orleans or wherever, so we do that. You get them on a bus, point them to [a local service

agency]. A lot of people I point to [the local service agency] have already been there or know about it. This week [there] is a woman and a two-year-old that is going to go over to [another local service agency]. I have a book in the truck full of resources that I could point people at, but that's about it.

As a result, Fellowship Outreach and other groups could only try to meet immediate, pressing needs, which, in turn, meant that group members became frustrated by seeing familiar faces and familiar problems week after week. The problem seemed insurmountable.

Volunteers with a more individualistic/color-blind understanding of homelessness sometimes had inflated expectations about what could be accomplished through charity. Providing for people's immediate needs, though important, does not address the structural barriers needed for people to exit homelessness—steady, fair-paying work; safe, affordable housing; and reliable transportation (Edin and Shaefer 2015).

Groups that viewed homelessness as the product of systemic inequalities were more aware of the limitations of volunteer work, frequently lamenting the inability to provide anything more than a band-aid. Some volunteers recognized that their efforts did not address the larger problems of institutionalized racism or an inadequate welfare system, while others believed that the constant need to provide basic services left them with little time and energy for collective action. Moreover, members of Citywide, Fam in the Streets, and Mercy House saw the city as unlikely to undertake meaningful action to help those living precariously.

Nevertheless, organizing and pressuring the city to make policy changes may be the most appropriate response available. If the goal is systemic change, coordinated collective-action efforts—intentional coalitions of activists, volunteer and professional service providers, and people who have experienced or are currently experiencing homelessness—likely have the greatest potential for success.

A number of scholars have written extensively about homeless social movements and resistance (Cress 1997; Cress and Snow 1996, 2000; Wagner 1993; Wagner and Cohen 1991; Wright 1997). Daniel M. Cress and David A. Snow (1996, 2000), for example, show that well-organized collective action that unites diverse community actors results in sustained political pressure. Collective action on behalf of the poor has promoted their voting rights, resulted in protection from the police, and increased access to services and housing (Cress and Snow 2000; B. A. Lee, Tyler, and Wright 2010; Rosenthal 1994; Wright 1997). Such outcomes may feel unlikely following Donald Trump's second presidential victory, and to be sure, economic instability and growing economic inequality may follow. However, sustained political pressure remains important, and not all politics are national. Fur-

ther social and political movements should focus on improved working conditions and wages, the provision of affordable housing, and the addition of a cash
safety net to the U.S. welfare system, all of which would both directly and indirectly reduce homelessness in the country.

A Need for More Reflexive Antiracist Service

Volunteers, activists, and social service providers interested in social and racial
justice but acting from privileged racial and class positions must realize that inequality is a two-sided coin. Privilege exists in relation to oppression, and race and
class are the result of ongoing and historical processes whereby racial identity and
(inter)actions are both influenced by and make up social structure (Blumer 1958;
Collins 2013; Delgado and Stefancic 2012; Omi and Winant 1994; Rosino 2017;
Winant 2004).

Reflexivity is necessary and a constant process. Volunteers should better situate their thoughts, beliefs, and (inter)actions within the prevailing social, political,
and economic contexts (Gouldner 1970). Volunteers who question their perceptions and critically reflect on how their actions and beliefs are viewed by others
may develop improved understandings of how to provide particular services. And
groups whose members understand the world through the frames of color blindness must more openly consider the existence and importance of racial oppression
and privilege (Jason and Epplen 2016; O'Brien 2001; Warren 2010).

However, awareness of racial inequality and privilege does not necessarily
translate into disruptive antiracist praxis. Exposure to critical perspectives on race
and whiteness does not preclude continued (and innovative) justification of white
supremacist systems (Endres and Gould 2009; Mueller 2017; Mueller and Washington 2021), and white allyship has clear limitations (Droogendyk et al. 2016;
Endres and Gould 2009; Hughey 2007; Sullivan 2014; Sumerau et al. 2021). Volunteers attempting to resist the comfort of racial ignorance do not necessarily situate themselves within broader systems of race, class, and housing. For many volunteers, race was something people of color had, while whiteness was the absence
of race. Questions about class concerned those living in poverty, not members of
the middle class. Problems with housing systems concerned residents of segregated Black neighborhoods or people without stable shelter, not people living in
"normal" circumstances. Race and class were most meaningful in explaining the
disadvantages faced by others (Croll 2013; Lewis 2004) rather than the advantages
enjoyed by the volunteers themselves.

Resolving the tension between whiteness and antiracism will not be an easy

feat. Social-justice-oriented volunteers, service providers, and activists undoubt-
edly face significant barriers. Racial group position necessarily informs people's
view of the world, providing a particular vantage point that informs and obstructs
the way people see, interpret, and interact with the surrounding world (Ahmed
2007; Feagin 2013; Mueller 2020). So how can whites effectively participate in antiracist discourse, service, and social movements?

One way of improving reflexivity and therefore altering service practices would
be to push volunteer discourse beyond discussion of sickness and sin. Because volunteers generally adopt their service group's outlook and approach, introducing
social justice ideals, encouraging alternative viewpoints, and practicing reflexivity
at the group level is likely to impact the ways individuals engage in service. Under
the right circumstances, within-group dialogue can lead people to antiracist identities (Feagin and O'Brien 2004; O'Brien and Korgen 2007). However, conversation between similarly positioned people has at best diminishing returns and at
worst can reproduce harmful tropes about marginalized groups while cementing
the worldview of those engaged in this discourse (Hughey 2007).

Evidence shows that service experiences or relationships with activists and/or
people of color may move some whites further down the path of color-consciousness and social-justice ideals (Allport 1954; Cress and Snow 1996, 2000; Knecht
and Martinez 2009; O'Brien and Korgen 2007; Sigelman and Welch 1993; Warren 2010; Reason and Evans 2007; Fingerhut and Hardy 2020). Thus, groups must
not remain racially homogenous. Diversifying volunteer and other service organizations, placing people of color in positions of leadership, and facilitating open
and honest dialogue between volunteers and service recipients may push volunteer work toward more effective modes of antiracist service and decenter white
logics (Bortree and Waters 2014).

This pathway also has its obstacles. For example, racial minorities may bear the
burden of antiracist work if whites are not willing to accept and reflect on their
role in the reproduction of unequal systems (al-Gharbi 2019; Sumerau et al. 2021).
Ultimately, antiracism needs to be understood as a continuous process, and total enlightenment can never be achieved (Hanchey 2018; Ray 2020). But service
opportunities can enable volunteers to grow as openly color-conscious antiracists
as they network with others with similar racial ideologies and social justice values and make connections outside their racial and class groups. These encounters
will inform their senses of self, others, and society moving forward (Feagin and
O'Brien 2004; Perry and Shotwell 2009).

Participant Demographics

TABLE 2
Volunteers Interviewed

	RACE	AGE	RELIGION	PLACE OF RESIDENCE	CLASS
Citywide Outreach					
Dominic	Asian	23		central corridor	upper-middle
Dorothea	white-Asian	18	Christian "in part"	central corridor	lower-middle
Fran	white	60	"believer"; Catholic	north city	working/middle
Gabriela	white	65		south city	middle
Giles	white	59	Methodist	metro east	lower-working
Joseph	white	76			upper-middle
Lucy	white				
Martha	white	63	Quaker	south city	middle
René	white	28		south city	middle
Simon	white	64	atheist	northwest suburb	middle
Tatiana	white	57	United Methodist	southwest suburb	middle
Vincent	white	41	nonreligious	west suburb	middle
Fam in the Streets					
Cecilia	Black	34	Christian	north suburb	lower
Germaine	Black	57	"child of God"	north suburb	middle
Margaret	white	58	Episcopalian	south city	middle
Quentin	white	55		south city	lower-middle
Regina	white	49	Episcopalian	south city	lower
Thomas	white	28	Catholic	north suburb	lower
Fellowship Outreach					
Agnes	white				
Alena	Black	37	nondenominational Christian	west suburb	middle
Bernard	white	42	"Bible only"; Christian	west suburb	middle
Claire	white	42	Christian	rural Missouri	middle
Elizabeth	Black	26	Christian	central corridor	lower-middle
Jude	white	68	"raised Catholic"; atheist	northwest suburb	middle
Martin	white	54	Christian	south city	upper-middle
Peter	white	51	"Jesus"	west suburb	working/ middle
Mercy House					
Adrian	Latinx	21	Catholic	central corridor	middle
Ambrose	white	20	Catholic		upper-middle
Barbara	white	41	spiritual	north city	upper-middle
Catherine	white	23	"there's something out there"		lower-middle
Christina	Black			north city	previously experienced homelessness

	RACE	AGE	RELIGION	PLACE OF RESIDENCE	CLASS
Mercy House (*continued*)					
Joan	white	24	Catholic	north city	
Paul	white	23		north city	middle
Rose	Black	36	nondenominational Christian metro east middle	metro east	middle
Sixtus		58	Catholic	north city	lower
Right Choice Ministry and Outreach					
John	white	40	nondenominational Christian	southwest suburb	working/middle
Lawrence	white	38	Christian	west suburb	middle
Teresa	white	35	Christian/ Spiritual	west suburb	middle
Veronica	white	32	nondenominational Christian	west suburb	upper-middle
Service House					
Anthony	Black	25	Episcopalian	north city	
Justin	white	23	Episcopalian	north city	upper-middle
Mary	white				
Preferred Not to Be Grouped					
Ana	white	23	Christian		lower-middle

TABLE 3
Unhoused People Interviewed

	LOCATION	AGE	RACE
Alexander	South Side	57	white
Andrew	North Side	38	Black
David	North Side	62	Black
Enos	East Side	58	white
Willie	East Side	48	white

TABLE 4
Referenced in Text but Not Interviewed

	LOCATION	AGE	RACE
Volunteers			
Aaron	Citywide	early middle age	white
Alfonso	Fam in the Streets	mid- to late 20s	Black
Britta	Right Choice	early middle age	Black
Dominic	Right Choice	early elderly	white
Gregory	Right Choice	early middle age	white
Julia	Mercy House	early middle age	Asian
Michael	Fellowship	middle age	white
Pauline	Right Choice	early middle age	Black
Raymond	Right Choice	middle age	white
Unhoused People			
Clark	South Side	early middle age	white
Gibby	East Side	middle age	white
Jed	South Side	middle age	Black
Kyle	East Side	middle age	white
Lance	South Side	mid- to late 20s	Black
Lou	downtown	middle age	white
Lynn	South Side	early middle age	white
Miss Alberta	downtown	late middle age	Black
Scott	North Side	middle age	Black
Stan	North Side	late middle age	white

NOTES

Introduction

1. In 1876, the state of Missouri officially split the City of St. Louis from St. Louis County, meaning that the two jurisdictions' governments, tax bases, and land areas do not overlap (Gordon 2008).

2. Barbara, Paul, and Bernard were each interviewed twice, while Cecelia and Thomas were interviewed together. For the demographics of the interviewees, see the appendix.

3. A few longtime Fellowship members mentioned that in previous versions of the group, this issue had arisen. The current leadership, however, was unconcerned about ensuring that the group maintained an explicitly Christian character. In fact, despite the clear importance of religious practice on a nightly basis, Peter regularly suggested that religion was not a central feature of the group.

Chapter 1

1. A branch of Citywide that I did not work with operates a number of semipermanent housing units for which tenants pay a small monthly rent.

2. The rules include safety precautions such as refraining from entering dwellings, avoiding interrupting illegal drug transactions, and leaving if they feel unsafe.

3. Mercy House published a quarterly newsletter that primarily featured op-ed-style essays, with each issue organized around a different theme. Some of these essays involved self-reflection, while others offered well-researched histories of local, regional, and national social issues such as displacement (gentrification), "Ferguson: Voices from the Movement," and climate change. The pieces generally had a progressive activist bent and attempted to engage with structural-level social issues either by situating the authors' experiences within larger social contexts or exploring the historical legacies of inequality.

Chapter 2

1. Fellowship and Right Choice generally focused on a small number of people, perhaps because of the desire for close connections or perhaps because the groups favored small, pre-

dominantly white gathering spots. As a result, volunteers' discussions featured a rather small cast of characters.

Chapter 3

1. She frequently cited this statistic, but its source is unclear. Based on my observations, she may have made a rough estimate based on her encounters.

2. Only 38 percent of whites indicated that Black disadvantage could be explained by the idea that "laws and institutions work against blacks more than other racial groups" (Croll 2013, 55).

3. The racial ideologies of those included in this study are explicitly color-conscious and antiracist. They openly acknowledged and grappled with the reality of racism, setting them apart from whites who claim not to notice race but in fact work to maintain systems of white supremacy through a supposed color blindness (Bonilla-Silva 2010). I use "color-conscious" here to draw attention to the notable difference between the whites featured in this chapter and color-blind whites, but descriptors such as "racism-conscious" or "racial-justice-oriented" would also be appropriate.

4. Writing in 1969, Day advocated the "teaching of revolution" by reading about Mahatma Gandhi, Che Guevara, and Ho Chi Minh, with the objective being to "begin now within the shell of the old to rebuild society" (Day 1969, 2).

Chapter 4

1. They were always excited when they saw the raccoons and occasionally criticized Stan for allowing them to reside there and for feeding them.

2. To preserve the original poem, "Alex" is the only name in this book that has not been replaced by a pseudonym.

3. The taking of photographs was common in most of the groups with which I worked, although Citywide explicitly asked volunteers not to do so. I never observed photos being taken by volunteers with Service House or Mercy House, perhaps because they are not outreach groups and the nature of their work was different. Members of Fam in the Streets did take photos, and the group's efforts were frequently featured on local news outlets, but volunteers with Right Choice and Fellowship more frequently took photos.

4. The latter images might also have represented an attempt to reproduce the "poor but happy" trope (Crossley 2012). However, these photos almost always included volunteers, I have coded these images as cases of volunteer relationship framing.

5. Articulating homeless or Black spaces as dangerous was far more common among color-blind groups. However, the theme existed to a lesser degree among social-justice-minded volunteer groups. Both Simon and Justin were members of groups that operated based on social and racial justice frameworks.

6. Bernard directly criticized not only American Black English but also young Black men, whom he described as the "Ebonics speaking, thug type[s]" who "wear [their] pants below [their] ass." Bernard's overt criticisms were unusual among research participants, who were much more likely to express their underlying expectations through coded talk and action.

REFERENCES

Ahmed, Sara. 2007. "A Phenomenology of Whiteness." *Feminist Theory* 8 (2): 149–68. https://doi.org/10.1177/1464700107078139.

Al-Gharbi, Musa. 2019. "Resistance as Sacrifice: Toward an Ascetic Antiracism." *Sociological Forum* 34 (s1): 1197–1216. https://doi.org/10.1111/socf.12544.

Allard, Scott W. 2009. *Out of Reach: Place, Poverty, and the New American Welfare State.* New Haven: Yale University Press.

Allport, Gordon. 1954. *The Nature of Prejudice.* Garden City, N.Y.: Doubleday.

Amster, Randall. 2003. "Patterns of Exclusion: Sanitizing Space, Criminalizing Homelessness." *Social Justice* 30 (1): 195–221.

———. 2008. *Lost in Space: The Criminalization, Globalization, and Urban Ecology of Homelessness.* New York: LFB Scholarly.

Anderson, Elijah. 2015. "The White Space." *Sociology of Race and Ethnicity* 1 (1): 10–21. https://doi.org/10.1177/2332649214561306.

Anderson, Kathryn Freeman. 2017. "Racial Residential Segregation and the Distribution of Health-Related Organizations in Urban Neighborhoods." *Social Problems* 64 (2): 256–76. https://doi.org/10.1093/socpro/spw058.

Apfelbaum, Evan P., Samuel R. Sommers, and Michael I. Norton. 2008. "Seeing Race and Seeming Racist? Evaluating Strategic Colorblindness in Social Interaction." *Journal of Personality and Social Psychology* 95 (4): 918–32. https://doi.org/10.1037/a0011990.

Appiah, K. Anthony, and Amy Gutmann. 1996. *Color Conscious: The Political Morality of Race.* Princeton: Princeton University Press.

Ashwood, J. Scott, Karishma R. Patel, David Kravitz, David M. Adamson, and M. Audrey Burnam. 2019. "Evaluation of the Homeless Multidisciplinary Street Team for the City of Santa Monica." Santa Monica, Calif.: Rand Corporation. https://www.rand.org/pubs/research_reports/RR2848.html.

Aviles de Bradley, Ann. 2015. "Homeless Educational Policy: Exploring a Racialized Discourse through a Critical Race Theory Lens." *Urban Education* 50 (7): 839–69. https://doi.org/10.1177/0042085914534861.

Aykanian, Amanda, and Wonhyung Lee. 2016. "Social Work's Role in Ending the Criminalization of Homelessness: Opportunities for Action." *Social Work* 61 (2): 183–85. https://doi.org/10.1093/sw/sww011.

Bauman, Zygmunt. 1998. *Globalization: The Human Consequences*. New York: Columbia University Press.

Bayat, Asef. 2010. *Life as Politics: How Ordinary People Change the Middle East*. ISIM Series on Contemporary Muslim Societies. Amsterdam: Amsterdam University Press.

Beckett, Katherine, and Steve Herbert. 2010. *Banished: The New Social Control in Urban America*. Oxford: Oxford University Press.

Beeman, Angie. 2022. *Liberal White Supremacy: How Progressives Silence Racial and Class Oppression*. Athens: University of Georgia Press.

Belcher, John R., and Bruce R. DeForge. 2012. "Social Stigma and Homelessness: The Limits of Social Change." *Journal of Human Behavior in the Social Environment* 22 (8): 929–46. https://doi.org/10.1080/10911359.2012.707941.

Benjaminsen, Lars, and Stefan Bastholm Andrade. 2015. "Testing a Typology of Homelessness across Welfare Regimes: Shelter Use in Denmark and the USA." *Housing Studies* 30 (6): 858–76. https://doi.org/10.1080/02673037.2014.982517.

Berg, Justin Allen. 2015. "Explaining Attitudes toward Immigrants and Immigration Policy: A Review of the Theoretical Literature." *Sociology Compass* 9 (1): 23–34. https://doi.org/10.1111/soc4.12235.

Berger, Peter L. 1990. *The Sacred Canopy: Elements of a Sociological Theory of Religion*. New York: Anchor.

Birmingham, Elizabeth. 1999. "Reframing the Ruins: Pruitt-Igoe, Structural Racism, and African American Rhetoric as a Space for Cultural Critique." *Western Journal of Communication* 63 (3): 291–309. https://doi.org/10.1080/10570319909374643.

Blouin, David D., and Evelyn M. Perry. 2009. "Whom Does Service Learning Really Serve? Community-Based Organizations' Perspectives on Service Learning." *Teaching Sociology* 37 (2): 120–35. https://doi.org/10.1177/0092055X0903700201.

Blumer, Herbert. 1958. "Race Prejudice as a Sense of Group Position." *Pacific Sociological Review* 1 (1): 3–7. https://doi.org/10.2307/1388607.

———. 1969. *Symbolic Interactionism: Perspective and Method*. Berkeley: University of California Press.

Bolger, Daniel. 2021. "The Racial Politics of Place in Faith-Based Social Service Provision." *Social Problems* 68 (3): 535–51. https://doi.org/10.1093/socpro/spz061.

———. 2022. "The Collective Construction of Need: Group Styles of Determining Deservingness in Christian Social Service Agencies." *Sociological Quarterly* 63 (1): 74–93. https://doi.org/10.1080/00380253.2020.1788468.

Bonilla-Silva, Eduardo. 2010. *Racism without Racists: Color-Blind Racism and the Persistence of Racial Inequality in America*. Lanham, Md.: Rowman and Littlefield.

Bonilla-Silva, Eduardo, Carla Goar, and David G. Embrick. 2006. "When Whites Flock Together: The Social Psychology of White Habitus." *Critical Sociology* 32 (2–3): 229–53. https://doi.org/10.1163/156916306777835268.

Bonnett, Alastair. 1996. "Anti-Racism and the Critique of 'White' Identities." *Journal of Ethnic and Migration Studies* 22 (1): 97–110. https://doi.org/10.1080/1369183X.1996.9976524.

Bortree, Denise Sevick, and Richard D. Waters. 2014. "Race and Inclusion in Volunteerism: Using Communication Theory to Improve Volunteer Retention." *Journal of Public Relations Research* 26 (3): 215–34. https://doi.org/10.1080/1062726X.2013.864245.

Brekhus, Wayne. 1998. "A Sociology of the Unmarked: Redirecting Our Focus." *Sociological Theory* 16 (1): 34–51. https://doi.org/10.1111/0735-2751.00041.

Brown, Melissa. 2017. "The Sociology of Antiracism in Black and White." *Sociology Compass* 11 (2): 1–11. https://doi.org/10.1111/soc4.12451.

Browne, Irene, and Joya Misra. 2003. "The Intersection of Gender and Race in the Labor Market." *Annual Review of Sociology* 29 (1): 487–513. https://doi.org/10.1146/annurev.soc.29.010202.100016.

Burdsey, Daniel. 2011. "That Joke Isn't Funny Anymore: Racial Microaggressions, Color-Blind Ideology and the Mitigation of Racism in English Men's First-Class Cricket." *Sociology of Sport Journal* 28 (3): 261–83. https://doi.org/10.1123/ssj.28.3.261.

Burke, Meghan A. 2012. *Racial Ambivalence in Diverse Communities: Whiteness and the Power of Color-Blind Ideologies*. Lanham, Md.: Lexington.

Butler, Shelley Ruth. 2012. "Curatorial Interventions in Township Tours." In *Slum Tourism: Poverty, Power, Ethics*, edited by Fabian Frenzel, Ko Koens, and Malte Steinbrink, 215–31. London: Routledge.

Cann, Colette N., and Erin McCloskey. 2017. "The Poverty Pimpin' Project: How Whiteness Profits from Black and Brown Bodies in Community Service Programs." *Race Ethnicity and Education* 20 (1): 72–86. https://doi.org/10.1080/13613324.2015.1096769.

Case, Kim A. 2012. "Discovering the Privilege of Whiteness: White Women's Reflections on Anti-Racist Identity and Ally Behavior." *Journal of Social Issues* 68 (1): 78–96. https://doi.org/10.1111/j.1540-4560.2011.01737.x.

Charities Aid Foundation. 2017. "CAF World Giving Index 2017: A Global View of Giving Trends." https://www.cafonline.org/docs/default-source/about-us-publications/cafworldgivingindex2017_2167a_web_210917.pdf.

Chhabra, Deepak, Robert Healy, and Erin Sills. 2003. "Staged Authenticity and Heritage Tourism." *Annals of Tourism Research* 30 (3): 702–19. https://doi.org/10.1016/S0160-7383(03)00044-6.

Christian, Michelle. 2019. "A Global Critical Race and Racism Framework: Racial Entanglements and Deep and Malleable Whiteness." *Sociology of Race and Ethnicity* 5 (2): 169–85. https://doi.org/10.1177/2332649218783220.

Christian, Michelle, Louise Seamster, and Victor Ray. 2019. "New Directions in Critical Race Theory and Sociology: Racism, White Supremacy, and Resistance." *American Behavioral Scientist* 63 (13): 1731–40. https://doi.org/10.1177/0002764219842623.

Clary, E. Gil, and Mark Snyder. 1999. "The Motivations to Volunteer: Theoretical and Practical Considerations." *Current Directions in Psychological Science* 8 (5): 156–59. https://doi.org/10.1111%2F1467-8721.00037.

Clayton, Patti H., and Sarah L. Ash. 2004. "Shifts in Perspective: Capitalizing on the Counter-Normative Nature of Service-Learning." *Michigan Journal of Community Service Learning* 11 (1): 59–70. http://hdl.handle.net/2027/spo.3239521.0011.106.

Clifford, Scott, and Spencer Piston. 2017. "Explaining Public Support for Counterproductive Homelessness Policy: The Role of Disgust." *Political Behavior* 39 (2): 503–25. https://doi.org/10.1007/s11109-016-9366-4.

Cloward, Richard A., and Frances Fox Piven. 1984. "Disruption and Organization." *Theory and Society* 13 (4): 587–99. https://doi.org/10.1007/bf00156904.

Collins, Patricia Hill. 2000. *Black Feminist Thought: Knowledge, Consciousness, and the Politics of Empowerment.* Rev. 10th anniv. ed. New York: Routledge.

———. 2013. *On Intellectual Activism.* Philadelphia: Temple University Press.

Conradson, David. 2003. "Spaces of Care in the City: The Place of a Community Drop-in Centre." *Social and Cultural Geography* 4 (4): 507–25. https://doi.org/10.1080/1464936 032000137939.

Conran, Mary. 2011. "They Really Love Me! Intimacy in Volunteer Tourism." *Annals of Tourism Research* 38 (4): 1454–73. https://doi.org/10.1016/j.annals.2011.03.014.

Corbin, Juliet, and Anselm Strauss. 2008. *Basics of Qualitative Research: Techniques and Procedures for Developing Grounded Theory.* Los Angeles: Sage.

Crane, Maureen, Kathleen Byrne, Ruby Fu, Bryan Lipmann, Frances Mirabelli, Alice Rota-Bartelink, Maureen Ryan, Robert Shea, Hope Watt, and Anthony M. Warnes. 2005. "The Causes of Homelessness in Later Life: Findings From a 3-Nation Study." *Journals of Gerontology: Series B* 60 (3): S152–59. https://doi.org/10.1093/geronb/60.3.S152.

Crenshaw, Kimberlé. 1991. "Mapping the Margins: Intersectionality, Identity Politics, and Violence against Women of Color." *Stanford Law Review* 43 (6): 1241–99. https://doi .org/10.2307/1229039.

Cress, Daniel M. 1997. "Nonprofit Incorporation among Movements of the Poor." *Sociological Quarterly* 38 (2): 343–60. https://doi.org/10.1111/j.1533-8525.1997.tb00481.x.

Cress, Daniel M., and David A. Snow. 1996. "Mobilization at the Margins: Resources, Benefactors, and the Viability of Homeless Social Movement Organizations." *American Sociological Review* 61 (6): 1089–1109. https://doi.org/10.2307/2096310.

———. 2000. "The Outcomes of Homeless Mobilization: The Influence of Organization, Disruption, Political Mediation, and Framing." *American Journal of Sociology* 105 (4): 1063–1104.

Croll, Paul R. 2013. "Explanations for Racial Disadvantage and Racial Advantage: Beliefs about Both Sides of Inequality in America." *Ethnic and Racial Studies* 36 (1): 47–74. https://doi.org/10.1080/01419870.2011.632426.

Crossley, Émilie. 2012. "Poor but Happy: Volunteer Tourists' Encounters with Poverty." *Tourism Geographies* 14 (2): 235–53. https://doi.org/10.1080/14616688.2011.611165.

Crowder, Kyle. 2000. "The Racial Context of White Mobility: An Individual-Level Assessment of the White Flight Hypothesis." *Social Science Research* 29 (2): 223–57. https://doi.org/10.1006/ssre.1999.0668.

Crowder, Kyle, and Scott J. South. 2008. "Spatial Dynamics of White Flight: The Effects of Local and Extralocal Racial Conditions on Neighborhood Out-Migration." *American Sociological Review* 73 (5): 792–812. https://doi.org/10.1177/000312240807300505.

Dakin, Andone, and Faith Karimi. 2017. "St. Louis Ex-Officer Acquitted in Fatal Shooting of Black Driver." *CNN* (blog), September 16. https://www.cnn.com/2017/09/15/us /jason-stockley-officer-shooting-verdict/index.html.

Day, Dorothy. 1969. "Sanctuary." *Catholic Worker Movement*, February, 1–2, 8..

Dei, George J. Sefa. 1996. "Critical Perspectives in Antiracism: An Introduction." *Canadian Review of Sociology* 33 (3): 247–67. https://doi.org/10.1111/j.1755-618X.1996.tb02452.x.

Delgado, Richard, and Jean Stefancic. 2012. *Critical Race Theory: An Introduction*. New York: New York University Press.

Delli Carpini, Michael X. 2000. "Gen.Com: Youth, Civic Engagement, and the New Information Environment." *Political Communication* 17 (4): 341–49. https://doi.org/10.1080/10584600050178942.

DeSante, Christopher D. 2013. "Working Twice as Hard to Get Half as Far: Race, Work Ethic, and America's Deserving Poor." *American Journal of Political Science* 57 (2): 342–56. https://doi.org/10.1111/ajps.12006.

DiTomaso, Nancy, Rochelle Parks-Yancy, and Corinne Post. 2003. "White Views of Civil Rights: Color Blindness and Equal Opportunity." In *White Out: The Continuing Significance of Racism*, 189–98. New York: Routledge.

Doane, Ashley W. 1997. "Dominant Group Ethnic Identity in the United States: The Role of 'Hidden' Ethnicity in Intergroup Relations." *Sociological Quarterly* 38 (3): 375–97. https://doi.org/10.1111/j.1533-8525.1997.tb00483.x.

Domínguez, Silvia, and Celeste Watkins. 2003. "Creating Networks for Survival and Mobility: Social Capital among African-American and Latin-American Low-Income Mothers." *Social Problems* 50 (1): 111–35. https://doi.org/10.1525/sp.2003.50.1.111.

Donley, Amy M., and James D. Wright. 2012. "Safer Outside: A Qualitative Exploration of Homeless People's Resistance to Homeless Shelters." *Journal of Forensic Psychology Practice* 12 (4): 288–306. https://doi.org/10.1080/15228932.2012.695645.

Dovey, Kim, and Ross King. 2012. "Informal Urbanism and the Taste for Slums." *Tourism Geographies* 14 (2): 275–93. https://doi.org/10.1080/14616688.2011.613944.

Droogendyk, Lisa, Stephen C. Wright, Micah Lubensky, and Winnifred R. Louis. 2016. "Acting in Solidarity: Cross-Group Contact between Disadvantaged Group Members and Advantaged Group Allies." *Journal of Social Issues* 72 (2): 315–34. https://doi.org/10.1111/josi.12168.

D'Souza, Dinesh. 1995. *The End of Racism: Principles for a Multiracial Society*. New York: Free Press.

Du Bois, W. E. B. 2015. *Souls of Black Folk*. Edited by Manning Marable. New York: Routledge.

Duneier, Mitchell. 1999. *Sidewalk*. New York: Farrar, Straus and Giroux.

Dunn, Tasha R. 2018. "Digging In: White Trash, Trailer Trash, and the (Im)Mobility of Whiteness." In *Interrogating the Communicative Power of Whiteness*, edited by Dawn Marie D. McIntosh, Dreama G. Moon, and Thomas K. Nakayama, 117–32. New York: Routledge.

Dürr, Eveline, and Rivke Jaffe. 2012. "Theorizing Slum Tourism: Performing, Negotiating and Transforming Inequality." *Revista Europea de Estudios Latinoamericanos y del Caribe/European Review of Latin American and Caribbean Studies* 93:113–23. http://www.jstor.org/stable/23294474.

Dyson, Peter. 2012. "Slum Tourism: Representing and Interpreting 'Reality' in Dharavi, Mumbai." *Tourism Geographies* 14 (2): 254–74. https://doi.org/10.1080/14616688.2011.609900.

Edgell, Penny, and Eric Tranby. 2007. "Religious Influences on Understandings of Racial Inequality in the United States." *Social Problems* 54 (2): 263–88. https://doi.org/10.1525/sp.2007.54.2.263.

Edin, Kathryn, and H. Luke Shaefer. 2015. *$2.00 a Day: Living on Almost Nothing in America*. New York: Mariner.

Einfeld, Aaron, and Denise Collins. 2008. "The Relationships between Service-Learning, Social Justice, Multicultural Competence, and Civic Engagement." *Journal of College Student Development* 49 (2): 95–109. https://doi.org/10.1353/csd.2008.0017.

Eliasoph, Nina. 2013. *The Politics of Volunteering*. Cambridge: Polity Press.

Elmasry, Mohamad Hamas, and Mohammed el-Nawawy. 2017. "Do Black Lives Matter?" *Journalism Practice* 11 (7): 857–75. https://doi.org/10.1080/17512786.2016.1208058.

Emerson, Michael O., and Christian Smith. 2000. *Divided by Faith: Evangelical Religion and the Problem of Race in America*. Oxford: Oxford University Press.

Endres, Danielle, and Mary Gould. 2009. "'I Am Also in the Position to Use My Whiteness to Help Them Out': The Communication of Whiteness in Service Learning." *Western Journal of Communication* 73 (4): 418–36. https://doi.org/10.1080/10570310903279083.

Ensign, J., and J. Santelli. 1997. "Shelter-Based Homeless Youth: Health and Access to Care." *Archives of Pediatrics and Adolescent Medicine* 151 (8): 817–23. doi:10.1001/archpedi.1997.02170450067011.

Erickson, Kurt. 2022. "Missouri Governor Signs Law Aimed at Cracking down on Homeless Camps." *St. Louis Post Dispatch*, June 30. https://www.stltoday.com/print/a-section/missouri-governor-signs-law-aimed-at-cracking-down-on-homeless-camps/article_08f6d0c5-e3ab-5bb6-a58a-fca9cc2f81d7.html.

Farley, John E. 1991. "Black-White Housing Segregation in the City of St. Louis: A 1988 Update." *Urban Affairs Quarterly* 26 (3): 442–50. https://doi.org/10.1177/004208169102600307.

———. 1995. "Race Still Matters: The Minimal Role of Income and Housing Cost as Causes of Housing Segregation in St. Louis, 1990." *Urban Affairs Review* 31 (2): 244–54. https://doi.org/10.1177/107808749503100207.

———. 2005. "Race, Not Class: Explaining Racial Housing Segregation in the St. Louis Metropolitan Area, 2000." *Sociological Focus* 38 (2): 133–50. https://doi.org/10.1080/00380237.2005.10571261.

Fazel, Seena, Vivek Khosla, Helen Doll, and John Geddes. 2008. "The Prevalence of Mental Disorders among the Homeless in Western Countries: Systematic Review and Meta-Regression Analysis." *PLoS Medicine* 5 (12): E225>. https://doi.org/10.1371/journal.pmed.0050225.

Feagin, Joe R. 2013. *The White Racial Frame*. New York: Routledge.

Feagin, Joe R., and Eileen O'Brien. 2004. *White Men on Race: Power, Privilege, and the Shaping of Cultural Consciousness*. Boston: Beacon Press.

Federico, Christopher M., and James Sidanius. 2002. "Sophistication and the Antecedents of Whites' Racial Policy Attitudes—Racism, Ideology, and Affirmative Action in America." *Public Opinion Quarterly* 66 (2): 145–76. https://doi.org/10.1086/339848.

Fingerhut, Adam W., and Emma R. Hardy. 2020. "Applying a Model of Volunteerism to Better Understand the Experiences of White Ally Activists." *Group Processes and Intergroup Relations* 23 (3): 344–60. https://doi.org/10.1177/1368430219837345.

Fisher, Dana R. 2006. *Activism, Inc.: How the Outsourcing of Grassroots Campaigns Is Strangling Progressive Politics in America*. Stanford, Calif.: Stanford University Press.

Foster-Bey, John. 2008. *Do Race, Ethnicity, Citizenship and Socio-Economic Status Determine*

Civic-Engagement? Medford, Mass.: Center for Information and Research on Civic Learning and Engagement, Tufts University. https://eric.ed.gov/?id=ED505266.

Frankenberg, Ruth. 1993. *White Women, Race Matters: The Social Construction of Whiteness.* Minneapolis: University of Minnesota Press.

———. 2001. "The Mirage of an Unmarked Whiteness." In *The Making and Unmaking of Whiteness*, edited by Birgit Brander Rasmussen, Eric Klinenberg, Irene J. Nexica, and Matt Wray, 72–96. Durham, N.C.: Duke University Press.

Freire-Medeiros, Bianca. 2013. *Touring Poverty.* London: Routledge.

Frenzel, Fabian. 2013. "Slum Tourism in the Context of the Tourism and Poverty (Relief) Debate." *Die Erde: Journal of the Geographical Society of Berlin* 144 (2): 117–28. https://doi.org/10.12854/erde-144-9.

———, ed. 2015. *Tourism and Geographies of Inequality: The New Global Slumming Phenomenon.* London: Routledge.

———. 2016. *Slumming It: The Tourist Valorization of Urban Poverty.* London: Zed.

Frenzel, Fabian, Ko Koens, Malte Steinbrink, and Christian M. Rogerson. 2015. "Slum Tourism: State of the Art." *Tourism Review International* 18 (4): 237–52. https://doi.org/10.3727/154427215X14230549904017.

Friedman, Bruce D. 2002. "Two Concepts of Charity and Their Relationship to Social Work Practice." *Social Thought* 21 (1): 3–19. https://doi.org/10.1300/J131v21n01_02.

Frisch, Thomas. 2012. "Glimpses of Another World: The Favela as a Tourist Attraction." *Tourism Geographies* 14 (2): 320–38. https://doi.org/doi.org/10.1080/14616688.2011.60 9999.

Froyum, Carissa. 2018. "'They Are Just Like You and Me': Cultivating Volunteer Sympathy." *Symbolic Interaction* 41 (4): 465–87. https://doi.org/10.1002/symb.357.

Gallagher, Charles A. 1995. "White Reconstruction in the University." *Socialist Review* 24 (1–2): 165–87.

———. 1997. "White Racial Formation: Into the 21st Century." In *Critical White Studies: Looking behind the Mirror*, edited by Richard Delgado and Jean Stefancic, 6–11. Philadelphia: Temple University Press.

———. 2003. "Color-Blind Privilege: The Social and Political Functions of Erasing the Color Line in Post Race America." *Race, Gender and Class* 10 (4): 22–37. https://www.jstor.org/stable/41675099.

Garfinkel, Harold. 1967. *Studies in Ethnomethodology.* Oxford: Blackwell.

Germann Molz, Jennie. 2017. "Giving Back, Doing Good, Feeling Global: The Affective Flows of Family Voluntourism." *Journal of Contemporary Ethnography* 46 (3): 334–60. https://doi.org/10.1177/0891241615610382.

Godfrey, Jane, Stephen L. Wearing, Nico Schulenkorf, and Simone Grabowski. 2019. "The 'Volunteer Tourist Gaze': Commercial Volunteer Tourists' Interactions with, and Perceptions of, the Host Community in Cusco, Peru." *Current Issues in Tourism* 23 (20): 2555–71. https://doi.org/10.1080/13683500.2019.1657811.

Goffman, Erving. 1959. *The Presentations of Self in Everyday Life.* New York: Pantheon.

———. 1967. *Interaction Ritual.* New York: Pantheon.

———. 1989. "On Fieldwork." *Journal of Contemporary Ethnography* 18 (2): 369–83. https://doi.org/10.1177/089124189018002001.

Gonzales, Ernest, Huei-Wern Shen, Yi Wang, Linda Sprague Martinez, and Julie Norstrand.

2016. "Race and Place: Exploring the Intersection of Inequity and Volunteerism among Older Black and White Adults." *Journal of Gerontological Social Work* 59 (5): 381–400. https://doi.org/10.1080/01634372.2016.1224787.

Goodman, Lisa A., Leonard Saxe, and Mary Harvey. 1991. "Homelessness as Psychological Trauma: Broadening Perspectives." *American Psychologist* 46 (11): 1219–25. https://doi .org/10.1037/0003-066X.46.11.1219.

Gordon, Colin. 2008. *Mapping Decline: St. Louis and the Fate of the American City*. Philadelphia: University of Pennsylvania Press.

Gouldner, Alvin W. 1970. *The Coming Crisis of Western Sociology*. New York: Basic Books.

Gowan, Teresa. 2010. *Hobos, Hustlers, and Backsliders: Homeless in San Francisco*. Minneapolis: University of Minnesota Press.

Greene, Melanie. 2014. "On the Inside Looking In: Methodological Insights and Challenges in Conducting Qualitative Insider Research." *Qualitative Report* 19 (29): 1–13. https://doi.org/10.46743/2160-3715/2014.1106.

Hackworth, Jason. 2012. *Faith Based: Religious Neoliberalism and the Politics of Welfare in the United States*. Athens: University of Georgia Press.

Hage, Ghassan. 2016. "Recalling Anti-Racism." *Ethnic and Racial Studies* 39 (1): 123–33. https://doi.org/10.1080/01419870.2016.1096412.

Hagerman, Margaret A. 2018. *White Kids: Growing Up with Privilege in a Racially Divided America*. New York: New York University Press.

Hall, Stuart, Chas Critcher, Tony Jefferson, John Clarke, and Brian Roberts. 1978. *Policing the Crisis: Mugging, the State, and Law and Order*. London: Palgrave.

Hanchey, Jenna N. 2018. "All of Us Phantasmic Saviors." *Communication and Critical/ Cultural Studies* 15 (2): 144–60. https://doi.org/10.1080/14791420.2018.1454969.

Harris, David R. 2001. "Why Are Whites and Blacks Averse to Black Neighbors?" *Social Science Research* 30 (1): 100–116. https://doi.org/10.1006/ssre.2000.0695.

Harrison, David. 2008. "Pro-Poor Tourism: A Critique." *Third World Quarterly* 29 (5): 851–68. https://doi.org/10.1080/01436590802105983.

Harrison, Lawrence E. 1992. *Who Prospers: How Cultural Values Shape Economic and Political Success*. New York: Basic Books.

Hartigan, John. 1997. "Establishing the Fact of Whiteness." *American Anthropologist* 99 (3): 495–505. https://doi.org/10.1525/aa.1997.99.3.495.

———. 1999. "Establishing the Fact of Whiteness." In *Race, Identity, and Citizenship: A Reader*, edited by Rodolfo D. Torres, Luis F. Mirón, and Jonathan Xavier Inda, 183–99. Malden, Mass.: Blackwell.

Hartmann, Douglas, Joseph Gerteis, and Paul R. Croll. 2009. "An Empirical Assessment of Whiteness Theory: Hidden from How Many?" *Social Problems* 56 (3): 403–24. https:// doi.org/10.1525/sp.2009.56.3.403.

Heathcott, Joseph. 2012. "Planning Note: Pruitt-Igoe and the Critique of Public Housing." *Journal of the American Planning Association* 78 (4): 450–51. https://doi.org/10.1080 /01944363.2012.737972.

Heathcott, Joseph, and MáIre Agnes Murphy. 2016. "Corridors of Flight, Zones of Renewal: Industry, Planning, and Policy in the Making of Metropolitan St. Louis, 1940–1980." *Journal of Urban History* 31 (2): 151–89. https://doi.org/10.1177/0096144204270715.

Helms, Janet E. 1997. "Toward a Model of White Racial Identity Development." In *College

Student Development and Academic Life: Psychological, Intellectual, Social and Moral Issues, edited by Karen Arnold and Ilda Carreiro King, 207–24. New York: Routledge.

Henry, Jacob. 2022. "Whiteness in Transit: The Racialized Geographies of International Volunteering." *Social and Cultural Geography* 23 (7): 1007–23. https://doi.org/10.1080/14649365.2020.1861642.

Henry, Meghan, Rain Watt, and Azim Shivji. 2016. *The 2016 Annual Homeless Assessment Report (AHAR) to Congress*. Washington, D.C.: U.S. Department of Housing and Urban Development.

Hernández, Kelly Lytle. 2017. *City of Inmates: Conquest, Rebellion, and the Rise of Human Caging in Los Angeles, 1771–1965*. Chapel Hill: University of North Carolina Press.

Herring, Chris. 2019. "Complaint-Oriented Policing: Regulating Homelessness in Public Space." *American Sociological Review* 84 (5): 769–800. https://doi.org/10.1177/0003122419872671.

Heyl, Barbara Sherman. 2001. "Ethnographic Interviewing." In *Handbook of Ethnography*, edited by Paul Atkinson, Amanda Coffey, Sara Delamont, John Lofland, and Lyn H. Lofland, 369–83. Thousand Oaks, Calif.: Sage.

Higbie, Frank Tobias. 2003. *Indispensable Outcasts: Hobo Workers and Community in the American Midwest, 1880–1930*. Urbana: University of Illinois Press.

Hoffman, Lisa, and Brian Coffey. 2008. "Dignity and Indignation: How People Experiencing Homelessness View Services and Providers." *Social Science Journal* 45 (2): 207–22. https://doi.org/10.1016/j.soscij.2008.03.001.

Hollander, Justin B., Karina Pallagst, Terry Schwarz, and Frank J. Popper. 2009. *Planning Shrinking Cities*. Rochester, N.Y.: Social Science Research Network. https://papers.ssrn.com/abstract=1616130.

"Homelessness." n.d. *StLouis-Mo.Gov*. Accessed March 4, 2020. https://www.stlouis-mo.gov/government/departments/mayor/initiatives/resilience/equity/opportunity/health-safety/homelessness.cfm.

Hopper, Elizabeth K., Ellen L. Bassuk, and Jeffrey Olivet. 2010. "Shelter from the Storm: Trauma-Informed Care in Homelessness Services Settings." *Open Health Services and Policy Journal* 3 (2): 80–100. https://benthamopenarchives.com/contents/pdf/TOHSPJ/TOHSPJ-3-80.pdf.

Hughey, Matthew W. 2007. "Racism with Antiracists: Color-Conscious Racism and the Unintentional Persistence of Inequality." *Social Thought and Research* 28:67–108. https://www.jstor.org/stable/23252122.

———. 2010. "The (Dis)Similarities of White Racial Identities: The Conceptual Framework of 'Hegemonic Whiteness.'" *Ethnic and Racial Studies* 33 (8): 1289–1309. https://doi.org/10.1080/01419870903125069.

———. 2012. *White Bound: Nationalists, Antiracists, and the Shared Meanings of Race*. Stanford, Calif.: Stanford University Press.

———. 2014. *The White Savior Film: Content, Critics, and Consumption*. Philadelphia: Temple University Press.

Hughey, Matthew W., David G. Embrick, and Ashley "Woody" Doane. 2015. "Paving the Way for Future Race Research: Exploring the Racial Mechanisms within a Color-Blind, Racialized Social System." *American Behavioral Scientist* 59 (11): 1347–57. https://doi.org/10.1177/0002764215591033.

Huguelet, Austin. 2023. "St. Louis Finishes Clearing Riverfront Homeless Encampment." *St. Louis Post Dispatch*, March 11. https://www.stltoday.com/news/local/government -politics/st-louis-finishes-clearing-riverfront-homeless-encampment /article_5e9a3c78-3a6e-57b7-a9c1-e3095bc664bb.html

Hunter, Marcus Anthony, and Zandria F. Robinson. 2016. "The Sociology of Urban Black America." *Annual Review of Sociology* 42:385–405. https://doi.org/10.1146 /annurev-soc-081715-074356.

Jason, Kendra, and Sarah Nell Epplen. 2016. "Interrogating Ourselves in a Racialized World: Using Personal Experience to Improve Students' Understanding of Racism." *Sociology of Race and Ethnicity* 2 (4): 584–90. https://doi.org/10.1177/2332649216660570.

Johnsen, Sarah, Paul Cloke, and Jon May. 2005. "Transitory Spaces of Care: Serving Homeless People on the Street." *Health and Place* 11 (4): 323–36. https://doi. org/10.1016/j.healthplace.2004.03.002.

Johnson, Walter. 2021. *The Broken Heart of America*. New York: Basic Books.

Katz, Michael B. 1993. "Reframing the 'Underclass' Debate." In *The "Underclass" Debate: Views from History*, 440–78. Princeton: Princeton University Press.

Kelley, Robin D. G. 1997. *Yo' Mama's Disfunktional ! Fighting the Culture Wars in Urban America*. Boston: Beacon Press.

Kendi, Ibram X. 2019. *How to Be an Antiracist*. New York: One World.

Kinder, Donald R., and Lynn M. Sanders. 1996. *Divided by Color: Racial Politics and Democratic Ideals*. Chicago: University of Chicago Press.

Kipp, Amy, Roberta Hawkins, and Noella J. Gray. 2021. "Gendered and Racialized Experiences and Subjectivities in Volunteer Tourism." *Gender, Place and Culture* 28 (1): 45–65. https://doi.org/10.1080/0966369X.2019.1708274.

Kirschenman, Joleen, and Kathryn M. Neckerman. 1991. "'We'd Love to Hire Them, But . . .': The Meaning of Race for Employers." In *The Urban Underclass*, edited by Christopher Jencks and Paul E. Peterson, 203–32. Washington, D.C.: Brookings Institution.

Knecht, Tom, and Lisa M. Martinez. 2009. "Humanizing the Homeless: Does Contact Erode Stereotypes?" *Social Science Research* 38 (3): 521–34. https://doi.org/10.1016 /j.ssresearch.2009.01.009.

Knowles, Eric D., Brian S. Lowery, Rosalind M. Chow, and Miguel M. Unzueta. 2014. "Deny, Distance, or Dismantle? How White Americans Manage a Privileged Identity." *Perspectives on Psychological Science* 9 (6): 594–609. https://doi .org/10.1177/1745691614554658.

Knowles, Eric D., Brian S. Lowery, Caitlin M. Hogan, and Rosalind M. Chow. 2009. "On the Malleability of Ideology: Motivated Construals of Color Blindness." *Journal of Personality and Social Psychology* 96 (4): 857–69. https://doi.org/10.1037/a0013595.

Kochel, Tammy R. 2015. *Assessing the Initial Impact of the Michael Brown Shooting and Police and Public Responses to It on St. Louis County Residents' Views about Police*. Carbondale: Southern Illinois University. https://core.ac.uk/download/pdf /60576809.pdf.

Kontogeorgopoulos, Nick. 2016. "Forays into the Backstage: Volunteer Tourism and the Pursuit of Object Authenticity." *Journal of Tourism and Cultural Change* 15 (5): 455–75. https://doi.org/10.1080/14766825.2016.1184673.

Kowal, Emma. 2015. *Trapped in the Gap: Doing Good in Indigenous Australia*. New York: Berghahn.

Krull, Ryan. 2023. "New Homeless Camp Sets Up within a Block of St. Louis City Hall." *Riverfront Times*, October 11. https://www.riverfronttimes.com/news /new-homeless-camp-sets-up-within-a-block-of-st-louis-city-hall-41025972.

Krysan, Maria. 2015. "Are We Color-Blind? A View from the Neighborhood." In *Reclaiming Integration and the Language of Race in the "Post-Racial" Era*, edited by Curtis L. Ivery and Joshua A. Bassett, 20–32. Lanham, Md.: Rowman and Littlefield.

Lasker, Judith. 2016. *Hoping to Help: The Promises and Pitfalls of Global Health Volunteering*. Ithaca: Cornell University Press.

Lawrence, Mark. 1995. "Rural Homelessness: A Geography without a Geography." *Journal of Rural Studies* 11 (3): 297–307. https://doi.org/10.1016/0743-0167(95)00025-I.

Lee, Barrett A., Kimberly A. Tyler, and James D. Wright. 2010. "The New Homelessness Revisited." *Annual Review of Sociology* 36: 501–21. https://doi.org/10.1146/ annurev-soc-070308-115940.

Lee, Young-joo, and Jeffrey L. Brudney. 2009. "Rational Volunteering: A Benefit-Cost Approach." *International Journal of Sociology and Social Policy* 29 (9/10): 512–30. https:// doi.org/10.1108/01443330910986298.

Lewis, Amanda E. 2001. "There Is No 'Race' in the Schoolyard: Color-Blind Ideology in an (Almost) All-White School." *American Educational Research Journal* 38 (4): 781–811. https://doi.org/10.3102/00028312038004781.

———. 2003. *Race in the Schoolyard: Negotiating the Color Line in Classrooms and Communities*. New Brunswick, N.J.: Rutgers University Press.

———. 2004. "'What Group?' Studying Whites and Whiteness in the Era of 'Color-Blindness.'" *Sociological Theory* 22 (4): 623–46. https://doi .org/10.1111/j.0735-2751.2004.00237.x.

Link, Bruce G., Sharon Schwartz, Robert Moore, Jo Phelan, Elmer Struening, Ann Stueve, and Mary Ellen Colten. 1995. "Public Knowledge, Attitudes, and Beliefs about Homeless People: Evidence for Compassion Fatigue?" *American Journal of Community Psychology* 23 (4): 533–55. https://doi.org/10.1007/bf02506967.

Lipsitz, George. 1995. "The Possessive Investment in Whiteness: Racialized Social Democracy and the 'White' Problem in American Studies." *American Quarterly* 47 (3): 369–87. https://doi.org/10.2307/2713291.

———. 1998. *The Possessive Investment in Whiteness: How White People Profit from Identity Politics*. Philadelphia: Temple University Press.

Lockhart, P. R. 2019. "Ferguson Changed How America Talks about Police Violence: 5 Years Later, Not Much Else Has Changed." *Vox* (blog), August 9. https://www.vox.com/identities/2019/8/9/20798921/ michael-brown-ferguson-uprising-police-violence-reform.

Lough, Benjamin J., and Janet Carter-Black. 2015. "Confronting the White Elephant: International Volunteering and Racial (Dis)Advantage." *Progress in Development Studies* 15 (3): 207–20. https://doi.org/10.1177/1464993415578983.

Loury, Glenn C. 2002. *The Anatomy of Racial Inequality*. Cambridge: Harvard University Press.

Lyon-Callo, Vincent. 2000. "Medicalizing Homelessness: The Production of Self-Blame and

Self-Governing within Homeless Shelters." *Medical Anthropology Quarterly* 14 (3): 328–45. https://doi.org/10.1525/maq.2000.14.3.328.

———. 2015. *Inequality, Poverty, and Neoliberal Governance: Activist Ethnography in the Homeless Sheltering Industry*. 2nd ed. Toronto: University of Toronto Press.

MacCannell, Dean. 1973. "Staged Authenticity: Arrangements of Social Space in Tourist Settings." *American Journal of Sociology* 79 (3): 589–603. https://doi.org/10.1086/225585.

———. 1992. *The Tourist: A New Theory of the Leisure Class*. New York: Schocken.

Main, Thomas. 1998. "How to Think about Homelessness: Balancing Structural and Individual Causes." *Journal of Social Distress and the Homeless* 7 (1): 41–54. https://doi.org/10.1023/A:1022966631533.

Manyara, Geoffrey, and Eleri Jones. 2007. "Community-Based Tourism Enterprises Development in Kenya: An Exploration of Their Potential as Avenues of Poverty Reduction." *Journal of Sustainable Tourism* 15 (6): 628–44. https://doi.org/10.2167/jost723.0.

Markowitz, Fred E., and Jeffrey Syverson. 2021. "Race, Gender, and Homelessness Stigma: Effects of Perceived Blameworthiness and Dangerousness." *Deviant Behavior* 42 (7): 919–31. https://doi.org/10.1080/01639625.2019.1706140.

Massey, Douglas S., Andrew B. Gross, and Mitchell L. Eggers. 1991. "Segregation, the Concentration of Poverty, and the Life Chances of Individuals." *Social Science Research* 20 (4): 397–420. https://doi.org/10.1016/0049-089X(91)90020-4.

Maxwell, Mark. 2023. "Mayor Jones Made 'Heavy-Handed' Threats to Cut Homeless Funding in 'Retaliation' against Critic, Lawsuit Alleges." KSDK, August 9. https://www.ksdk.com/article/news/politics/mayor-tishaura-jones-heavy-handed-threats-cut-homeless-funding-retaliation-critic-lawsuit-alleges-st-patrick-center/63-cb0085eb-8f96-4dd2-987a-f25ae40d7260.

May, Reuben A. Buford. 2014. *Urban Nightlife: Entertaining Race, Class, and Culture in Public Space*. New Brunswick, N.J.: Rutgers University Press.

Mayorga-Gallo, Sarah. 2019. "The White-Centering Logic of Diversity Ideology." *American Behavioral Scientist* 63 (13): 1789–1809. https://doi.org/10.1177/0002764219842619.

McDermott, Monica. 2006. *Working-Class White : The Making and Unmaking of Race Relations*. Berkeley: University of California Press.

McDermott, Monica, and Frank L. Samson. 2005. "White Racial and Ethnic Identity in the United States." *Annual Review of Sociology* 31: 245–61. https://doi.org/10.1146/annurev.soc.31.041304.122322.

McGraw, Sarah A., Mary Jo Larson, Susan E. Foster, Marilyn Kresky-Wolff, Elizabeth M. Botelho, Emily A. Elstad, Ana Stefancic, and Sam Tsemberis. 2010. "Adopting Best Practices: Lessons Learned in the Collaborative Initiative to Help End Chronic Homelessness (CICH)." *Journal of Behavioral Health Services and Research* 37 (2): 197–212. https://doi.org/10.1007/s11414-009-9173-3.

McIntosh, Alison J., and Anne Zahra. 2007. "A Cultural Encounter through Volunteer Tourism: Towards the Ideals of Sustainable Tourism?" *Journal of Sustainable Tourism* 15 (5): 541–56. https://doi.org/10.2167/jost701.0.

McIntosh, Peggy. 1989. "White Privilege: Unpacking the Invisible Knapsack." *Peace and Freedom*, July–August, 10–12. https://www.nationalseedproject.org/key-seed-texts/white-privilege-unpacking-the-invisible-knapsack.

Mead, George Herbert. 1962. *Mind, Self, and Society*. Chicago: University of Chicago Press.

Mead, Lawrence M. 1992. *The New Politics of Poverty: The Nonworking Poor in America*. New York: Basic Books.

Meehan, Mary. 2019. "Unsheltered and Uncounted: Rural America's Hidden Homeless." NPR Morning Edition (blog), July 4. https://www.npr.org/sections/health-shots/2019/07/04/736240349/in-rural-areas-homeless-people-are-harder-to-find-and-to-help.

Meschkank, Julia. 2011. "Investigations into Slum Tourism in Mumbai: Poverty Tourism and the Tensions between Different Constructions of Reality." *GeoJournal* 76 (1): 47–62. DOI:10.1007/s10708-010-9401-7.

Miles, Mattheu B., and A. Michael Huberman. 1984. *Qualitative Data Analysis: A Sourcebook of New Methods*. Beverly Hills, Calif.: Sage.

Mills, C. Wright. 2000. *The Sociological Imagination*. Oxford: Oxford University Press.

Minca, Claudio. 2000. "'The Bali Syndrome': The Explosion and Implosion of 'Exotic' Tourist Spaces." *Tourism Geographies* 2 (4): 389–403. https://doi.org/10.1080/146166800750035503.

Mitchell, Don. 2020. *Mean Streets: Homelessness, Public Space, and the Limits of Capital*. Athens: University of Georgia Press.

Mitchell, Don, and Nik Heynen. 2009. "The Geography of Survival and the Right to the City: Speculations on Surveillance, Legal Innovation, and the Criminalization of Intervention." *Urban Geography* 30 (6): 611–32. https://doi.org/10.2747/0272-3638.30.6.611.

Moffitt, Robert A. 2015. "The Deserving Poor, the Family, and the U.S. Welfare System." *Demography* 52 (3): 729–49. https://doi.org/10.1007/s13524-015-0395-0.

Moller, Stephanie, Evelyne Huber, John D. Stephens, David Bradley, and François Nielsen. 2003. "Determinants of Relative Poverty in Advanced Capitalist Democracies." *American Sociological Review* 68 (1): 22–51. https://doi.org/10.2307/3088901.

Moynihan, Daniel Patrick. 1965. *The Negro Family—The Case for National Action*. Washington, D.C.: U.S. Department of Labor, Office of Policy Planning Research.

Mueller, Jennifer C. 2017. "Producing Colorblindness: Everyday Mechanisms of White Ignorance." *Social Problems* 64 (2): 219–38. https://doi.org/10.1093/socpro/spw061.

———. 2020. "Racial Ideology or Racial Ignorance? An Alternative Theory of Racial Cognition." *Sociological Theory* 38 (2): 142–69. https://doi.org/10.1177/0735275120926197.

Mueller, Jennifer C., and DyAnna K. Washington. 2021. "Anticipating White Futures: The Ends-Based Orientation of White Thinking." *Symbolic Interaction* 45 (1): 3–26. https://doi.org/10.1002/symb.563.

Musick, Marc A., and John Wilson. 2008. *Volunteers: A Social Profile*. Bloomington: Indiana University Press.

Myers, Kristen A. 2005. *Racetalk : Racism Hiding in Plain Sight*. Lanham, Md.: Rowman and Littlefield.

National Law Center on Homelessness and Poverty. 2017. *Don't Count on It: How the HUD Point-in-Time Count Underestimates the Homelessness Crisis in America*. https://homelesslaw.org/wp-content/uploads/2018/10/HUD-PIT-report2017.pdf.

Newitz, Annalee, and Matthew Wray. 1996. "What Is 'White Trash'? Stereotypes and Economic Conditions of Poor Whites in the U.S." *Minnesota Review* 47 (1): 57–72.

Newman, Katherine S., and Rebekah Peeples Massengill. 2006. "The Texture of Hardship: Qualitative Sociology of Poverty, 1995–2005." *Annual Review of Sociology* 32: 423–46. https://doi.org/10.1146/annurev.soc.32.061604.123122.

Norton, Michael I., Samuel R. Sommers, Evan P. Apfelbaum, Natassia Pura, and Dan Ariely. 2006. "Color Blindness and Interracial Interaction: Playing the Political Correctness Game." *Psychological Science* 17 (11): 949–53. https://doi.org/10.1111/j.1467-9280.2006.01810.x.

O'Brien, Eileen. 2001. *Whites Confront Racism: Antiracists and Their Paths to Action*. Lanham, Md.: Rowman and Littlefield.

———. 2009. "From Antiracism to Antiracisms." *Sociology Compass* 3 (3): 501–12. https://doi.org/10.1111/j.1751-9020.2009.00206.x.

O'Brien, Eileen, and Kathleen Odell Korgen. 2007. "It's the Message, Not the Messenger: The Declining Significance of Black-White Contact in a 'Colorblind' Society*." *Sociological Inquiry* 77 (3): 356–82. https://doi.org/10.1111/j.1475-682X.2007.00197.x.

Oladipo, Gloria. 2023. "Alarm as U.S. States Pass 'Very Concerning' Anti-Homeless Laws." *The Guardian*, January 5. https://www.theguardian.com/us-news/2023/jan/05/us-states-homelessness-laws-alarm.

Omi, Michael. 2001. "(E)Racism: Emerging Practices of Antiracist Organizations." In *The Making and Unmaking of Whiteness*, edited by Birgit Brander Rasmussen, Eric Klinenberg, Irene J. Nexica, and Matt Wray, 266–93. Durham, N.C.: Duke University Press.

Omi, Michael, and Howard Winant. 1994. *Racial Formation in the United States: From the 1960s to the 1990s*. 2nd ed. New York: Routledge.

Osborne, Melissa. 2019. "Who Gets 'Housing First'? Determining Eligibility in an Era of Housing First Homelessness." *Journal of Contemporary Ethnography* 48 (3): 402–28. https://doi.org/10.1177/0891241617753289.

Paradies, Yin. 2016. "Whither Anti-Racism?" *Ethnic and Racial Studies* 39 (1): 1–15. https://doi.org/10.1080/01419870.2016.1096410.

Parr, H. 2000. "Interpreting the 'Hidden Social Geographies' of Mental Health: Ethnographies of Inclusion and Exclusion in Semi-Institutional Places." *Health and Place* 6 (3): 225–37. https://doi.org/10.1016/S1353-8292(00)00025-3

Parsell, Cameron, and Mitch Parsell. 2012. "Homelessness as a Choice." *Housing, Theory and Society* 29 (4): 420–34. https://doi.org/10.1080/14036096.2012.667834.

Perry, Pamela, and Alexis Shotwell. 2009. "Relational Understanding and White Antiracist Praxis." *Sociological Theory* 27 (1): 33–50. https://doi.org/10.1111/j.1467-9558.2009.00337.x.

Pew Research Center. 2021. *Deep Divisions in Americans' Views of Nation's Racial History—and How To Address It*. August. https://www.pewresearch.org/politics/2021/08/12/deep-divisions-in-americans-views-of-nations-racial-history-and-how-to-address-it/.

Phelan, Jo, Bruce G. Link, Ann Stueve, and Robert E. Moore. 1995. "Education, Social Liberalism, and Economic Conservatism: Attitudes toward Homeless People." *American Sociological Review* 60 (1): 126–40. https://doi.org/10.2307/2096349.

Pho, Yvon H. 2008. "The Value of Volunteer Labor and the Factors Influencing Participation: Evidence for the United States from 2002 through 2005." *Review of Income and Wealth* 54 (2): 220–36. https://doi.org/10.1111/j.1475–4991.2008.00271.x.

Plaut, Victoria C., Kecia M. Thomas, and Matt J. Goren. 2009. "Is Multiculturalism or Color Blindness Better for Minorities?" *Psychological Science* 20 (4): 444–46. https://doi.org/10.1111/j.1467-9280.2009.02318.x.

Purser, Gretchen, and Brian Hennigan. 2017. "'Work as unto the Lord': Enhancing Employability in an Evangelical Job-Readiness Program." *Qualitative Sociology* 40 (1): 111–33. https://doi.org/10.1007/s11133-016-9347-2.

Putnam, Robert D. 2000. *Bowling Alone: The Collapse and Revival of American Community*. New York: Simon and Schuster.

Ray, Victor. 2019. "A Theory of Racialized Organizations." *American Sociological Review* 84 (1): 26–53. https://doi.org/10.1177/0003122418822335.

———. 2020. "Antiracism Is a Constant Struggle." *Contexts*, July 20. https://contexts.org/articles/antiracism-is-a-constant-struggle/.

Raymond, Eliza Marguerite, and C. Michael Hall. 2008. "The Development of Cross-Cultural (Mis)Understanding through Volunteer Tourism." *Journal of Sustainable Tourism* 16 (5): 530–43. https://doi.org/10.1080/09669580802159610.

Reardon, Kenneth M. 2000. "An Experiential Approach to Creating an Effective Community-University Partnership: The East St. Louis Action Research Project." *Cityscape* 5 (1): 59–74. https://resolver.scholarsportal.info/resolve/1936007x/v05i0001/59_aeatcaeslarp.xml.

Reason, Robert D., and Nancy J. Evans. 2007. "The Complicated Realities of Whiteness: From Color Blind to Racially Cognizant." *New Directions for Student Services* 2007 (120): 67–75. https://doi.org/10.1002/ss.258.

Reutter, Linda I., Miriam J. Stewart, Gerry Veenstra, Rhonda Love, Dennis Raphael, and Edward Makwarimba. 2009. "'Who Do They Think We Are, Anyway?' Perceptions of and Responses to Poverty Stigma." *Qualitative Health Research* 19 (3): 297–311. https://doi.org/10.1177/1049732308330246.

Robinson, James W. 2009. "American Poverty Cause Beliefs and Structured Inequality Legitimation." *Sociological Spectrum* 29 (4): 489–518. https://doi.org/10.1080/02732170902904681.

Rodriguez, Nelson M., and Leila E. Villaverde. 2000. *Dismantling White Privilege: Pedagogy, Politics, and Whiteness*. New York: Lang.

Rogers, Laura E. 2017. "'Helping the Helpless Help Themselves': How Volunteers and Employees Create a Moral Identity while Sustaining Symbolic Boundaries within a Homeless Shelter." *Journal of Contemporary Ethnography* 46 (2): 230–60. https://doi.org/10.1177/0891241615603450.

Rosenthal, Robert. 1994. *Homeless In Paradise: A Map of the Terrain*. Philadelphia: Temple University Press.

Rosino, Michael L. 2017. "Dramaturgical Domination: The Genesis and Evolution of the Racialized Interaction Order." *Humanity and Society* 41 (2): 158–81. https://doi.org/10.1177/0160597615623042.

Rossi, Peter H. 1989. *Down and Out in America: The Origins of Homelessness*. Chicago: University of Chicago Press.

Rotolo, Thomas, John Wilson, and Mary Elizabeth Hughes. 2010. "Homeownership and Volunteering: An Alternative Approach to Studying Social Inequality and Civic Engagement." *Sociological Forum* 25 (3): 570–87. https://doi.org/10.1111/j.1573–7861.2010.01196.x.

Roy, Ananya. 2011. "Slumdog Cities: Rethinking Subaltern Urbanism." *International Journal of Urban and Regional Research* 35 (2): 223–38. https://doi.org/10.1111/j.1468–2427.2011.01051.x.

Saguy, Tamar, John F. Dovidio, and Felicia Pratto. 2008. "Beyond Contact: Intergroup Contact in the Context of Power Relations." *Personality and Social Psychology Bulletin* 34 (3): 432–45. https://doi.org/10.1177/0146167207311200.

Samson, Frank L. 2013. "Multiple Group Threat and Malleable White Attitudes towards Academic Merit." *Du Bois Review: Social Science Research on Race* 10 (1): 233–60. https://doi.org/10.1017/S1742058X1300012X.

Saussure, Ferdinand de. 2011. *Course in General Linguistics*. Translated by Wade Baskin. Edited by Perry Meisel and Haun Saussy. New York: Columbia University Press.

Schanzer, Bella, Boanerges Dominguez, Patrick E. Shrout, and Carol L. M. Caton. 2007. "Homelessness, Health Status, and Health Care Use." *American Journal of Public Health* 97 (3): 464–69. https://doi.org/10.2105/AJPH.2005.076190.

Scheyvens, Regina. 2001. "Poverty Tourism." *Development Bulletin—Australian Development Studies Network* 55:18–21. https://www.researchgate.net/publication/303697583_Poverty_Tourism.

———. 2007. "Exploring the Tourism-Poverty Nexus." *Current Issues in Tourism* 10 (2–3): 231–54. https://doi.org/10.2167/cit318.0.

Schneider, Matthew Jerome. 2018. "Exotic Place, White Space: Racialized Volunteer Spaces in Honduras." *Sociological Forum* 33 (3): 690–711. https://doi.org/10.1111/socf.12439.

Schofield, Janet Ward. 2002. "Increasing the Generalizability of Qualitative Research." In *The Qualitative Researcher's Companion*, edited by A. Michael Huberman and Matthew B. Miles, 171–203. Thousand Oaks, Calif.: Sage.

Schuman, Howard, Charlotte Steeh, and Lawrence Bobo. 1985. *Racial Attitudes in America: Trends and Interpretations*. Cambridge: Harvard University Press.

Sekula, Allan. 1981. "The Traffic in Photographs." *Art Journal* 41 (1): 15–25. https://doi.org/10.2307/776511.

———. 1982. "On the Invention of Photographic Meaning." In *Thinking Photography*, edited by Victor Burgin, 84–109. London: Macmillan Education UK.

Sherry, Mark. 2008. "Insider/Outsider Status." In *The Sage Encyclopedia of Qualitative Research Methods*, edited by Lisa M. Given, 433. Los Angeles: Sage.

Sidanius, Jim, and Felicia Pratto. 1999. *Social Dominance: An Intergroup Theory of Social Hierarchy and Oppression*. Cambridge: Cambridge University Press.

Sigelman, Lee, and Susan Welch. 1993. "The Contact Hypothesis Revisited: Black-White Interaction and Positive Racial Attitudes." *Social Forces* 71 (3): 781–95. https://doi.org/10.1093/sf/71.3.781.

Simpson, Kate. 2004. "'Doing Development': The Gap Year, Volunteer-Tourists and a

Popular Practice of Development." *Journal of International Development* 16 (5): 681–92. https://doi.org/10.1002/jid.1120.

Sin, Harng Luh. 2009. "Volunteer Tourism—'Involve Me and I Will Learn'?" *Annals of Tourism Research* 36 (3): 480–501. https://doi.org/10.1016/j.annals.2009.03.001.

Skocpol, Theda. 1997. "The Tocqueville Problem: Civic Engagement in American Democracy." *Social Science History* 21 (4): 455–79. https://doi.org/10.1017/S0145553200017818.

———. 1999. "Advocates without Members: The Recent Transformation of American Civic Life." In *Civic Engagement in American Democracy*, edited by Theda Skocpol and Morris P. Fiorina, 461–510. Washington, D.C.: Brookings Institution Press.

Smith, Curtis, and Ernesto Castañeda-Tinoco. 2019. "Improving Homeless Point-in-Time Counts: Uncovering the Marginally Housed." *Social Currents* 6 (2): 91–104. https://doi.org/10.1177/2329496518812451.

Snow, David A., and Leon Anderson. 1993. *Down on Their Luck: A Study of Homeless Street People*. Berkeley: University of California Press.

Snyder, Mark, and Allen M. Omoto. 2008. "Volunteerism: Social Issues Perspectives and Social Policy Implications." *Social Issues and Policy Review* 2 (1): 1–36. https://doi.org/10.1111/j.1751-2409.2008.00009.x.

Somers, Margaret R., and Fred Block. 2005. "From Poverty to Perversity: Ideas, Markets, and Institutions over 200 Years of Welfare Debate." *American Sociological Review* 70 (2): 260–87. https://doi.org/10.1177/000312240507000204.

Steinbrink, Malte. 2012. "'We Did the Slum!' Urban Poverty Tourism in Historical Perspective." *Tourism Geographies* 14 (2): 213–34. https://doi.org/10.1080/14616688.2012.633216.

Stuart, Forrest. 2016. *Down, out, and under Arrest: Policing and Everyday Life in Skid Row*. Chicago: University of Chicago Press.

Sullivan, Shannon. 2014. *Good White People: The Problem with Middle-Class White Anti-Racism*. Albany: SUNY Press.

Sumerau, J. E., TehQuin D. Forbes, Eric Anthony Grollman, and Lain A. B. Mathers. 2021. "Constructing Allyship and the Persistence of Inequality." *Social Problems* 68 (2): 358–73. https://doi.org/10.1093/socpro/spaa003.

Thompson, Becky. 2001. *A Promise and a Way Of Life: White Antiracist Activism*. Minneapolis: University of Minnesota Press.

Thornhill, Ted. 2019. "We Want Black Students, Just Not You: How White Admissions Counselors Screen Black Prospective Students." *Sociology of Race and Ethnicity* 5 (4): 456–70. https://doi.org/10.1177/2332649218792579.

Tiessen, Rebecca. 2012. "Motivations for Learn/Volunteer Abroad Programs: Research with Canadian Youth." *Journal of Global Citizenship and Equity Education* 2 (1). http://journals.sfu.ca/jgcee/index.php/jgcee/article/view/57.

Tochluk, Shelly. 2010. *Witnessing Whiteness: The Need to Talk about Race and How to Do It*. 2nd ed. Lanham, Md.: Rowman and Littlefield.

Toro, Paul A., Carolyn J. Tompsett, Sylvie Lombardo, Pierre Philippot, Hilde Nachtergael, Benoit Galand, Natascha Schlienz, Nadine Stammel, Yanélia Yabar, Marc Blume, Linda MacKay, and Kate Harvey. 2007. "Homelessness in Europe and the United States: A

Comparison of Prevalence and Public Opinion." *Journal of Social Issues* 63 (3): 505–24. https://doi.org/10.1111/j.1540-4560.2007.00521.x.

Tranby, Eric, and Douglas Hartmann. 2008. "Critical Whiteness Theories and the Evangelical 'Race Problem': Extending Emerson and Smith's Divided by Faith." *Journal for the Scientific Study of Religion* 47 (3): 341–59. https://doi.org/10.1111/j.1468-5906.2008.00414.x.

Tsai, Jack, Crystal Y. S. Lee, Thomas Byrne, Robert H. Pietrzak, and Steven M. Southwick. 2017. "Changes in Public Attitudes and Perceptions about Homelessness between 1990 and 2016." *American Journal of Community Psychology* 60 (3–4): 599–606. https://doi.org/10.1002/ajcp.12198.

Tsai, Jack, Crystal Y. S. Lee, Jianxun Shen, Steven M. Southwick, and Robert H. Pietrzak. 2019. "Public Exposure and Attitudes about Homelessness." *Journal of Community Psychology* 47 (1): 76–92. https://doi.org/10.1002/jcop.22100.

Underhill, Megan R. 2019. "'Diversity Is Important to Me': White Parents and Exposure-to-Diversity Parenting Practices." *Sociology of Race and Ethnicity* 5 (4): 486–99. https://doi.org/10.1177/2332649218790992.

Urry, John. 1990. *The Tourist Gaze: Leisure and Travel in Contemporary Societies.* London: Sage.

———. 1992. "The Tourist Gaze 'Revisited.'" *American Behavioral Scientist* 36 (2): 172–86. https://doi.org/10.1177/0002764292036002005.

———. 1996. "Tourism, Culture, and Social Inequality." In *The Sociology of Tourism: Theoretical and Empirical Investigations,* edited by Yiorgos Apostolopoulos, Andrew Yiannakis, and Stella Leivadi, 115–33. London: Routledge.

U.S. Census Bureau. 2018. *U.S. Census Bureau QuickFacts: United States.* July 1. https://www.census.gov/quickfacts/fact/table/US/PST045218.

———. 2019a. *U.S. Census Bureau QuickFacts: St. Louis City, Missouri (County)."* July 1. https://www.census.gov/quickfacts/stlouiscitymissouricounty.

———. 2019b. *U.S. Census Bureau QuickFacts: St. Louis County, Missouri.* July 1. https://www.census.gov/quickfacts/stlouiscountymissouri.

———. 2020. *U.S. Census Bureau QuickFacts: St. Louis City, Missouri.* April 1. https://www.census.gov/quickfacts/fact/table/stlouiscitymissouri/POP010220.

U.S. Department of Housing and Urban Development (HUD). 2017a. *Continuum of Care Homeless Assistance Programs Homeless Populations and Subpopulations: MO-501 St. Louis City CoC.* https://www.hudexchange.info/resource/reportmanagement/published/CoC_PopSub_CoC_MO-501-2017_MO_2017.pdf.

———. 2017b. *Continuum of Care Homeless Assistance Programs Homeless Populations and Subpopulations: MO-501 St. Louis County CoC.* https://www.hudexchange.info/resource/reportmanagement/published/CoC_PopSub_CoC_MO-500-2017_MO_2017.pdf.

———. 2019a. *Continuum of Care Homeless Assistance Programs Homeless Populations and Subpopulations: MO-501 St. Louis City CoC.* https://files.hudexchange.info/reports/published/CoC_PopSub_CoC_MO-501-2019_MO_2019.pdf.

———. 2019b. *Continuum of Care Homeless Assistance Programs Homeless Populations and Subpopulations: MO-501 St. Louis County CoC.* https://files.hudexchange.info/reports/published/CoC_PopSub_CoC_MO-500-2019_MO_2019.pdf.

———. 2022a. *Continuum of Care Homeless Assistance Programs Homeless Populations and Subpopulations: MO-501 St. Louis City CoC*. https://files.hudexchange.info/reports/published/CoC_PopSub_CoC_MO-501-2022_MO_2022.pdf.

———. 2022b. *Continuum of Care Homeless Assistance Programs Homeless Populations and Subpopulations: MO-501 St. Louis County CoC*. https://files.hudexchange.info/reports/published/CoC_PopSub_CoC_MO-500-2022_MO_2022.pdf.

U.S. Department of Labor, Bureau of Labor Statistics. 2016. *Volunteering in the United States, 2015*. February 25. https://www.bls.gov/news.release/volun.nr0.htm.

VanHeuvelen, Tom. 2014. "The Religious Context of Welfare Attitudes." *Journal for the Scientific Study of Religion* 53 (2): 268–95. https://doi.org/10.1111/jssr.12118.

Vera, Hernán, and Andrew M. Gordon. 2003. *Screen Saviors: Hollywood Fictions of Whiteness*. Lanham, Md.: Rowman and Littlefield.

Wacquant, Loïc. 2002. "Scrutinizing the Street: Poverty, Morality, and the Pitfalls of Urban Ethnography." *American Journal of Sociology* 107 (6): 1468–1532. https://doi.org/10.1086/340461.

Wagner, David. 1993. *Checkerboard Square: Culture and Resistance in a Homeless Community*. Boulder, Colo.: Routledge.

Wagner, David, and Marcia B. Cohen. 1991. "The Power of the People: Homeless Protesters in the Aftermath of Social Movement Participation." *Social Problems* 38 (4): 543–61. https://doi.org/10.2307/800570.

Warren, Mark R. 2010. *Fire in the Heart: How White Activists Embrace Racial Justice*. Oxford: Oxford University Press.

Wasserman, Jason Adam, and Jeffrey M. Clair. 2010. *At Home on the Street: People, Poverty, and a Hidden Culture of Homelessness*. Boulder, Colo.: Rienner.

Weber, Max. 2011. *The Protestant Ethic and the Spirit of Capitalism*. Translated by Stephen Kalberg. Rev. ed. New York: Oxford University Press.

Weiss, Robert S. 1994. *Learning from Strangers: The Art and Method of Qualitative Interview Studies*. New York: Free Press.

Wellman, David T. 1993. *Portraits of White Racism*. 2nd ed. Cambridge: Cambridge University Press.

Willse, Craig. 2015. *The Value of Homelessness: Managing Surplus Life in the United States*. Minneapolis: University of Minnesota Press.

Wilson, George. 1996. "Toward a Revised Framework for Examining Beliefs about the Causes of Poverty." *Sociological Quarterly* 37 (3): 413–28. https://doi.org/10.1111/j.1533-8525.1996.tb00746.x.

Wilson, John. 2012. "Volunteerism Research: A Review Essay." *Nonprofit and Voluntary Sector Quarterly* 41 (2): 176–212. https://doi.org/10.1177/0899764011434558.

Wilson, Thomas C. 2006. "Whites' Opposition to Affirmative Action: Rejection of Group-Based Preferences as Well as Rejection of Blacks." *Social Forces* 85 (1): 111–20. https://doi.org/10.1353/sof.2006.0148.

Wilson, William Julius. 1987. *The Truly Disadvantaged: The Inner City, the Underclass, and Public Policy*. Chicago: University Of Chicago Press.

Wiltz, Teresa. 2015. "States Struggle with 'Hidden' Rural Homelessness." *Pew Charitable Trusts* (blog), June 26. http://bit.ly/1KdMtwj.

Winant, Howard. 2004. *The New Politics Of Race: Globalism, Difference, Justice.* Minneapolis: University of Minnesota Press.

Wright, Talmadge. 1997. *Out of Place: Homeless Mobilizations, Subcities, and Contested Landscapes.* Albany: SUNY Press.

Yi, Jacqueline, Nathan R. Todd, and Yara Mekawi. 2019. "Racial Colorblindness and Confidence in and Likelihood of Action to Address Prejudice." *American Journal of Community Psychology* 65 (3–4): 407–22. https://doi.org/10.1002/ajcp.12409.

Zinn, Howard. 1980. *A People's History of the United States.* New York: Harper and Row.

Zuberi, Dan. 2006. *Differences That Matter: Social Policy and the Working Poor in the United States and Canada.* Ithaca: Cornell University Press.

INDEX

www.ingramcontent.com/pod-product-compliance
Lightning Source LLC
Chambersburg PA
CBHW032353280326
41935CB00008B/562

Volunteering is typically thought of as an act of altruism, yet there are power dynamics embedded in volunteer-service recipient relationships, especially when volunteers operate from privileged positions. Following six grassroots homeless service organizations in St. Louis, Missouri, Matthew Schneider unpacks the tensions between race, class, urban space, and volunteerism. Volunteers are well intentioned and provide vital, life-saving services. However, *Serving the Street* explores how many of these same volunteer groups helped to reproduce racialized stigma and stereotypes about poverty, homelessness, and marginal urban space through volunteer practices that bordered on "poverty tourism." If our goal is to make communities more inclusive and equitable, this book suggests a need for greater self-reflection, even among well-intentioned, social-justice-oriented volunteers.

"*Serving the Street* is a richly researched ethnography that adds to the burgeoning studies that focus on how well-intentioned whiteness reproduces durable inequalities. The lessons learned here are valuable for social-justice-oriented individuals and groups in that it implicitly questions the degree to which white allies can participate in antiracist social movements or day-to-day action where whiteness is simultaneously invisible and omnipresent." —Daina Cheyenne Harvey, professor of sociology and anthropology, College of the Holy Cross

"Deeply researched and richly informed by the literature, Schneider takes us somewhere new—the hearts and minds of class-privileged white volunteers assisting the unhoused in St. Louis. *Serving the Street* powerfully exposes the tension between volunteers' good intentions and their lack of racial and class reflexivity, revealing how a helping hand isn't always as helpful as we imagine." —Megan R. Underhill, associate professor of sociology, University of North Carolina Asheville

Matthew Jerome Schneider is an assistant professor of sociology at the University of North Carolina Wilmington, a collaborating professor with the Nippon Foundation Ocean Nexus Center, and the codirector of the Sustainability, Equity, and Action Laboratory. Situated in the areas of race and racism, environmental sociology, urban sociology, and community and civic engagement, his work has appeared in numerous outlets including *Qualitative Sociology, Sociological Forum, Radical Teacher, Environmental Justice,* and *Inside Higher Ed.*

Cover design: Amanda Weiss
Cover image: Adapted from photo by Paul Sableman;
https://www.flickr.com/photos/pasa/5652581092/
Author photo: Brian F. O'Neill

Sociology
of Race and
Ethnicity

ISBN 978-0-8203-7537-3
90000

9 780820 375373

The University of Georgia Press
Athens, Georgia 30602   *www.ugapress.org*